THE TOTEM

and other poetic musings

All My Best
to both of you.

Cheers.

Edmond Bruneau

ISBN: 978-1-936769-01-8
Library of Congress Control Number: 2016910210

Cover Design: Edmond Bruneau
Painting: Francis Sly

About the Front Cover

The Totem, painted by Francis Sly, was his wedding gift to my parents, Pierre and Bernadine Bruneau. It was displayed proudly on a wall in our living room and remained there until they moved to a new home during my first year of college. The poem, *The Totem*, appears in this book on page 9.

For Aubrey and Nathan –
you will always be
my daughter and son
no matter how old you become.
Thank you both for
continually surpassing
my high expectations.

FORWARD

It's always difficult to decide how to arrange one's poems for a book. Do you coordinate the poems by subject matter? Prose versus rhyme? Serious or whimsical? Alphabetical by title?

When I produce an album, I come from the old school philosophy that one song should lead to another for the ultimate listening experience. That means blending the different styles so an hour-long sit is more compelling than tedious.

I have attempted to do the same with this book's poem arrangement. A serious poem or two and then perhaps something lighter, maybe a smile along the way. It's my hope that if a reader desires to digest the book in one sitting, the poetry order will be more unexpected than predictable – with enough diversity to keep it interesting until the end.

Also, this time I added a photo when I thought It would enhance the experience – including the original letter sent to my parents from my substitute high school poetry class teacher.

Another departure is the addition of one short story close to the end of the book. Since the cover has a native american icon, I thought the tale fit into the context quite naturally.

Finally, I want to thank Donna Lange who is always the first to listen or read what I believe is a finished poem. Her penchant for correct grammar and understandable content make our impromptu editing sessions a loving and essential process that always improves the work.

The poems are better polished with her help. I am, as always, forever in her debt.

TABLE OF CONTENTS

EDMOND BRUNEAU

The Totem

As far back as I can remember,
the Totem was proudly displayed
by my parents in our living room.
It was an original oil painted by Francis Sly
who gave it to them as a wedding gift.
Growing up with it, I looked at it differently
than I would if seeing it in an art gallery.
It was part of our family. Part of the décor.
Providing splashes of color against
the robin egg blue walls,
solid grey wool carpeting
and the flickering black and white television.

At least once as a child,
I asked about the painting.
Dad said the artist used an indian blanket
as a backdrop.
He draped his coat on a table and painted the
totem with a gold charger plate behind it.
It really didn't answer my question, but I was
too young to articulate what I wanted to know.
*Why did the totem have long bunny ears
and buck teeth?*
*Where did the necklace of berries and seeds
come from?*
*Did the repeated symbol on the indian blanket
have meaning?*
What made the artist want to paint this still life?
And perhaps most important, *why did my
parents think this strange painting was beautiful?*
That's really what I wanted to know.

And now, over fifty years later,
I look at a photo of that painting
and it reminds me of Mom
knitting a sweater in the armchair
and Dad taking a catnap on the couch.
It reminds me of my youth. Simpler days.
When a buck-toothed totem painting
gave a sense of sophistication
to a rural country home.

In Our Nature

Cloud our skies
with polluted pride
because it's
in our nature.

Muddy our water
with disregard
because it's
in our nature.

Cut the trees
with reckless ease
because it's
in our nature.

Kill the bees
with apathy
because it's
in our nature.

Warm the planet.
Raise the seas.
Take it all –
leave nothing to leave.
Mother Earth is
sadly diseased –
because it's
in our nature.

Perception is Reality

I observe the world
and define my own reality.
That is my truth.
And my humility.
When someone else
owns a contrary opinion,
I realize
it came into being
through different insight.
I have no reason
to contest another's view,
as long as nothing
hinders mine.

I'm not opposed
to altering my perception.
Expanding my mind.
Learning new things.
Bridging other's observations
with my own,
painting hybrid panoramas
with genuine authenticity.

There is no universal truth.
No absolutes.
Winsome warriors
wish there were.
But we are all different,
unique filters
that sift and distill data.
Custom fit attire
we all wear devoutly.
Choosing our own gospel
over any naked truth.

I Think

My imagination makes me human and makes me a fool;
it gives me all the world and exiles me from it."
– Ursula K. Le Guin

I think.
Sometimes, perhaps,
a bit too much.
My imagination takes
me on journeys
far beyond the planets and stars.
And accompanies me
when I walk out to the mailbox.
I think.
About the future.
What lies ahead.
What tomorrow will bring.
And the fear of being redundant.
I think.
About my role here.
Light worker.
Consumer.
Peaceful warrior.
Am I a pebble thrown
causing ripples
reaching points unknown?
Here to teach or here to learn?
Maybe a bit of both.
If my imagination makes me a fool,
let the jesting begin.
If it makes me human,
I'll take that as a compliment.
It gives me the world,
the solar system, the universe.
And I'll be damned to let it
dismiss my purpose
into just taking up space on this planet.

Costco Dogs

My father in his eighties
would venture out
three or four times a week
in Bothell evening traffic
and drive four miles
to the closest Costco.

He'd take his walker
out of the car and
proceed to the food court
where he would order a
$1.50 quarter-pound hotdog
with complimentary
20-ounce fountain drink.

Then, onto the condiment area
to slather the all-beef frankfurter
with yellow mustard and white onions –
locate a table, park his walker,
and devour the exquisite sausage –
his delectable dining delight.

I once bought him a pack of
the very same Costco hotdogs
so he could enjoy the taste treat
in the comfort and safety of home.
They remained unopened in his freezer.

Perhaps, it was his dinnertime adventure.
Maybe it was because they're only $1.50.
Or possibly he just had a hankering
for that forbidden hot dog haven.
I worried about him driving there
so frequently at his age
in the heavy cosmopolitan traffic.

It wasn't the traffic that killed him,
but an inoperable bowel obstruction.

As the Crow Cries

Black bird caws
from treetop –
demanding attention,
voicing concern.
I don't have an inkling
what this clever bird
is trying to say.
Is it a warning
for our well being?
Or an inert babble about
the arrival of spring?
Whatever the message,
crow conveys
with conviction.
An important bulletin
for someone.
A constant reminder
that nature communicates
through its unique language.
A perspective
different than our own.
Next time you hear
crow calling,
pretend the
dispatch is for you.
Interpret the cries
as words to the wise.
A sign
of things to come.

Next Step

When life hands you lemons
you're supposed to make lemonade.
But what if it's a pomegranate?
Or day old loaf of bread?
These all are
motivations
to move beyond
where you are now.
Displace your comfort zone.
Clean out one's metaphysical closet.
Start a new chapter.
Sing a new song.
Rattle your routine.
Turn strangers into friends.
Invite chaos in
for a conversation.
Corral bad habits
and brand them anew
before releasing them
back into the wild.
Consider change
as opportunity.
Make misfortune
a lonely widow.
You are the one
who takes the
next step on your journey.
Toast the bread,
eat the fruit and
drink the lemonade.

Surprise yourself.

Pneumonia

During my entire second grade
my mother was in bed.
Her heart ravaged by
rheumatic fever in her teens –
Pneumonia compromised
her health exponentially.

Bed rest and large doses
of oral penicillin was the
doctor's advice. There were
whispers she might not make it.
It was something I had to
wrap my head around
in order to keep going to school
day after day. I was seven.

This was surely the most difficult
thing my mother had ever dealt with.
Square dancer. Bowler. Gardener.
Exercise enthusiast. Working out to
a segment on a local news program
called *Telescope*
and to the fabulous Jack Lalanne
in front of our black and white TV.

Confined to the bedroom.
Stripped of many
parental duties she loved.
My grandfather planted seeds
in the garden that spring.
I wondered who would tend to it.

There's a famous family story
about my father coming home
from swing shift at Boeing and
finding a roast my mother had
laid out for him to prepare.
He mistook it for a steak,
broiled it and ate the whole thing
before he went to bed.

She was a fighter.
Even in her darkest moments.
As spring came to an end,
she spent less time in bed
and began to build up
her endurance by swimming
in the local pool – eventually
becoming a Water Safety Instructor.

Third grade came around and Mom
was back doing all the same things
before she got sick. It would
still be years before she could stop
the heavy doses of medication.
But as she emerged from the disease,
she became a different person –
grateful for life and determined to give back.
She spent her next 18 years helping
the mentally handicapped with swimming
and other recreational activities.

Her serious bout with pneumonia
lead to something special and miraculous –
Leaving a big footprint on
the lives of many others.

Staff photo by Sally Tonkin

'Bernie' Bruneau works with one of her swimming students, Joel Damski, in the Juanita pool.

'Bernie' retires

Handicapped expert takes her first summer off in 18 years

The Easterner

The publication board was
conducting Spring interviews
for the year-long editor position
of the campus newspaper.
Me, a lowly freshman.
Cub reporter. Current editor
of the *Pearce Hall Bullsheet*
under the alias Perry White.
It was an honor normally awarded
to some deserving journalist
while they completed their senior year.
I arranged for my interview anyway.
What could it hurt?

I recall defiantly putting my feet up on the desk,
answering their questions
and submitting my vision for the paper's future.
After a week of deliberation,
the publication board made their choice
from all the qualified and worthy candidates.
To the shock of the entire campus,
including myself, they picked me.

The current editor was outraged.
The associate editor was her choice
for heir apparent. She would not
take this outcome lying down.
A special student council meeting was arranged
to right this obvious wrong.
With only a few days to prepare my case
for this conspicuous kangaroo court, I collected
letters from friends, teachers and the northwest
executive director of the Boy Scouts of America
who had presented my eagle scout award.

The crowd murmured a lynching disposition.
The student body president presided over the
standing room only council chambers,
my stack of character testimonials next to him.
He quieted the crowd and cut to the chase –
explaining that while it was commendable
I was a responsible student, had good character
and was even an eagle scout,

none of those factors were relevant
to the point at hand:
Did my editorial appointment
violate any of the rules,
terms or conditions
set forth by the student council
or the publications board?
His three words deflated all cries for justice.
"It did not."

That Fall, I began my year-long appointment
as editor of *The Easterner* for $45 a week.
The first sophomore to ever hold the position.
I chose a senior as my associate editor
who was also working part-time
at United Press International.
Together, we forged a weekly newspaper
certainly different than in years past –
testing boundaries, exploring new ideas
and reporting on – and sometimes
creating our own controversy.
It couldn't have been a better year.

(A special salute to John Allen, who was the student body
president when it all occurred - and now owns a wonderful
wine shop in Spokane, WA called **Vino**. An example of
The Easterner newspaper can be found on page 130)

The Paths We Choose

Most people who knew my father
didn't know he wanted to be a doctor.
As fate would have it, he got married at 19
and providing for his family
took precedence over
a long, difficult and expensive
college education. Instead,
he learned how to upholster furniture.
It paid the bills.
But I always thought not becoming a doctor
was one of his greatest regrets.
He had the emotional and
mental disposition for it.
If my sister or I got a deep sliver,
he was our go-to guy. He would
prepare a warm wash rag with hot water
and slowly fish out the long thin piece of wood
with a pair of tweezers, careful not to
have it break somewhere down the line
and require more extensive surgery.
He had a gentle bedside manner.
After completing his task and
patching us up, my mother
would always remind us that
"He wanted to be a doctor, you know."
I would ask, "Then why didn't he?"
She would only say,
"Things just didn't work out that way."
When I'd scrape my knee or bang my elbow –
Or if our cat got a broken leg –
it was a great relief for us to know
we had someone who had wanted
to be a doctor in the house
but chose to be a father instead.

Good Old Days

I lament the good old days.
When the front door was never locked,
even when we left home for awhile.

Languishing on a warm summer day –
without the burden and responsibility
of being continually tethered
via phone, text and email.

Adults voted in curtained booths
with a resolute belief
their participation in elections
was key to the power of freedom.

Families spent evenings removing
end tips of green beans for canning.
Television gave us four channels
in glorious black and white.

Thinking about those simpler times
makes me wonder just how far
we've ascended.

Or, if we've actually traded minutia
for long lost peace-of-mind.

No More Cats

Donna and I made a promise to each other.
No more cats. Until at least the
feline population became significantly less.
She brought 15 cats, a dog and two fish tanks
when we moved in together in 2009.
We were down to nine cats last year
when a stray kept coming around.
Skittish. Watching us from 20-30 feet away.
Looking hungry and thin.
Donna started leaving food out
and a month later, she could briefly pet it.
In another month, I could as well.
"Cami" adopted us. How could I refuse
to bring him into our tribe?

Then last November,
at the beginning of my three mile walk,
I heard a little meow up in a tree.
This little cat quickly climbed down
and began doing figure eights
around my shoes.
As I proceeded with my stroll,
it began to follow me.
Trotted along beside me.
Run ahead and then wait for me to catch up.
This went on for the entire three miles.
As I walked down our driveway, "Tami"
followed and waltzed right into the house.
"No more cats," Donna exclaimed. *"Ha!"*

Cami and Tami

Invisible

Why do you elude me
my fair weather friend?
My garden needs tending
and your neglect offends.

I phone and leave a message.
Hope you'll return the call.
Yet, you still remain absent
as if I'm not here at all.

It seems so dark and murky.
This indifference. This aversion.
Clouds with zero visibility.
A ghost and not a person.

I want to believe it's an aberration.
A faux pas. A momentary lapse.
Our past still prized and precious.
The future in our grasp.

Your avoidance. Your evasion.
May it serve you well.
I refuse to serve your passiveness.
What happens, only time will tell.

Debeaking

I remember it vividly because of the smell.
As a child, it was the first time I experienced
the aroma of burning flesh. It was putrid.
A side of the egg farm business
I must have been sheltered from, until then.

At a certain age, layer hens begin
feather pecking, aggression and
cannibalism when in close confinement.
The solution was to trim off the
upper portion of the beak using
an electrically heated blade
in a beak trimming machine,
providing a self-cauterizing cut.

Like on many farms, when extra help is needed,
family comes to the call. Mom and dad
were part of the process that
looked like a bucket brigade –
only with chickens instead of pails.
That year, I had a job as well.
At a certain part of the line,
I would dip a fork-like needle
into a brown liquid and
stab it into the hen's wing –
a vaccination to keep her healthy.

Unfortunately, it was also close to the smell.
And the chicken cluck screams
when debeaking was executed.
After a while, I remember asking to leave
and escape the stench and shrieks.
My grandfather gave me a glance of disdain,
but my grandmother understood,
dispatching me to the kitchen
to retrieve the prepared sandwiches.
When I returned, my younger sister
had taken over the vaccinations.
Farm kids grow up differently
than city kids, I think.

Want of a Nail

For the want of a nail the shoe was lost,
For the want of a shoe the horse was lost,
For the want of a horse the rider was lost,
For the want of a rider the battle was lost,
For the want of a battle the kingdom was lost,
And all for the want of a horseshoe-nail.

– Benjamin Franklin

For want of an email, the facts were lost.
For want of the facts, the source was lost.
For want of the source, truth was lost.
For want of the truth, belief was lost.
For want of belief, existence was lost.

Perhaps we should go back to
writing letters again.

Category 4 Vacation

Two weeks after 9/11
we set off on our adventure
planned more than six months in advance.
A seventeen day Panama Canal cruise
from Los Angeles to Tampa.
Few people yet had the courage to fly
and LAX was a ghost town.
It was ridiculously easy to find a cab
to take us to the cruise terminal.
We got into a long line, hearing
boarding had been delayed
because of a bomb threat.
Not a good omen.
After a few hours, decks were cleared
and boarding resumed.
As the ship departed for Cabo San Lucas
the captain announced over the loudspeaker
that there may be some rough weather ahead.
Rumors began to circulate among the passengers.
Someone said it might be a hurricane.
If it was, I thought, the captain would
turn the ship around and wait it out
in quieter waters. He didn't.
He thought he could sail around it.
He couldn't.
Instead, he drove us right into it.
Hurricane Juliette hit us the next day.
A category 4 event. 145 mile an hour winds.
And us, smack in the middle of it
on the unforgiving high seas of the Pacific.
Three days of horror and hell
watching the boat soar to a wave's crest
and disappear into a wall of water sinkhole.
Older passengers donned their life jackets
clogging the stairways. murmuring
to each other in panic and fear.
Portholes on the seventh floor
looked like front loader washing machines.
Some windows broke out on the eleventh.
The official advice was to stay calm,
don't use the elevators and don't go outside.

The ship remained somewhat in composure,
still offering normal dining, shows and nightlife –
but lacking the requisite passenger enthusiasm.
Three days passed and Juliette finally subsided.
We were all looking forward to Cabo San Lucas
to be rid our sea legs and kiss the dry land.
Sadly, our wait would be two days more
because there was no longer a dock in Cabo.
80 passengers got off the boat in Acapulco
and found other transportation home.
After that, we watched as the boat was mended –
windows replaced, pool tiles fixed,
all while cruising to our next stop –
finally reaching the sleepy calm waters
of the Panama Canal.
We were safe and steady now.
Warm sunshine and light breezes.
Hearts eventually leaving our throats.
Craving the comfort of the Caribbean.
Feeling damn lucky to be alive.

Sacred Heart Samurai

An ordinary morning west to east
waiting at the stoplight
at Northwest Boulevard.
Piloting my dark metallic blue
1986 Suzuki Samuri hardtop –
a nimble little four wheel drive
that worked as a daily driver
or climbed terrain like a mountain goat.

Light turned green.
Proceeded into the intersection.
only to see the silver 1981 Chrysler Le Baron
smack into my passenger side
from the corner of my eye.
It was estimated the blue-haired grandmother
was driving 45 miles an hour
and never applied her brakes.
Samurai bounced straight up into the air
and with support of angel wings,
guided back on its four tires 45 feet away.
Le Baron continued its barrage –
ironically through the plate glass window
of an auto parts store across the street.

I remember seeing the in-dash car radio
rocket past me upon impact
and fly out the back window.
All the glass in the car shattered,
some landing on my face and in my eyes.
I could squint, but didn't want the
chards to do damage. Located my phone
and called my wife,
letting her know what happened.

The ambulance came quickly and
rushed me to Sacred Heart Hospital.
Paramedics and emergency room doctors
carefully pulled particles from my eyes
and checked for other damage.
My seat belt cracked a rib
and the accident made the local evening news.
Samurai was totaled.

My angels protected me, once again.
I am forever cautious
and pause now for a second or two
before proceeding through
a changed-to-green light.

An Author's Apparatus

At first, I just used pencil on paper.
Lines scratched out, others erased
and re-written, darker,
covering the light grey blur left behind
from the worn pink pencil top.

Then I scored my parents hand-me-down.
A sixty pound electronic typing monster
built to withstand a nuclear holocaust.
I remember the roaring whir of the motor
upon engaging the "on" switch –
the loud snap of each letter's arm
forcing its impression on
the unsuspecting paper –
the defiant robotic carriage return
snapping back in place, locked and loaded,
ready to execute the next line
of punches and jabs.

Upon high school graduation, my parents
gave me a portable electric Smith-Corona –
aluminum cast in baby blue with white keys.
Twenty pounds in a soft leatherette case.
It was my roommate in college, my companion.
With me on those sullen, cerebral evenings
when the poetic muse stayed the night.
Course assignments enlisted it to duty,
presenting my work with its sharp, clear salute.

Used an IBM Selectric on my first job.
Miracle of modern engineering. Quiet. Precise.
With all the letters on one rotating ball
and an erase feature on the keyboard.
Misspell a word and correct without white-out.
Revolutionary.

Bought a Canon version of the Selectric in 1980
and began my own business. A couple years
later I discovered my Canon could be
converted to a printer
connected to one of those newfangled
personal computers.

Now I could compose on the computer and
store the contents on a floppy disc.
Fix my mistakes. Organize my thoughts.
Print and reprint originals.
Modify and revise
without having to type
the whole thing over again.
Once hooked, I never looked back.

Today, I write on my desktop computer.
Or on my three pound laptop.
Or on my less-than-a-pound tablet.
Print on the ink-jet or send via email
with a thousand available fonts.

My writing journey has gone from
horse and buggy to visiting Mars
in the course of my lifetime.
However, when a thought comes to mind,
a blank sheet of paper and
a pencil with a pink eraser
still works just fine.

Pray for Rain

I had forgotten what I like
about springtime best:

When pollen season is over.

Then I can wake up
without my eyes glued shut
and peer out the window
at the glorious morning sunrise.

I won't need to keep
a box of tissues handy
to capture the constant drip
of fluid flowing from my
already irritated nostrils.

Better yet, I won't have to take medicine
to sooth my sore, itchy throat
and I can retreat to a
normal sleeping pattern
to get a decent evening's rest
without coughing and wheezing
during all hours of the night.

Perhaps it's the pine pollen
or the bright green confetti
giddily tossed from the maples.
Maybe the box elder blooms
or the sycamore spores.

It could even be the grass
just mowed on Friday.
Maybe ragweed growing wild
in the field next door.
Honestly, I don't really care
which culprit causes me so much grief.
I beg this springtime infliction to pass –
as it will, eventually,
yielding the growth and beauty
spring possesses once this anomaly is over.

I pray for rain.

Chameleon

Matches his environment.
Camouflage. Adapt. Stealth.
But do we know the real deal?
Does he even know himself?

Is there ever a time
when truth becomes revealed?
Observe who he actually is
without appearances concealed?

How long does it take
for the worm to turn?
For a façade to crumble
and reality confirmed?

It's protection, you know.
A shield for his soul.
A way to survive in disguise –
the actual never to show.

It's tragic, this man of mystery.
Keeping all his roles straight.
Ends when someone sees through it
and the charlatan finds his fate.

Don't weep for the chameleon.
Don't pity his pathetic whim.
He hides as he can't face the truth
or let others really see him.

The Attic

At our house
we store stuff we don't use
but are not ready to throw away
in the attic.

Out of sight. Out of mind.
It's an interesting behavior
many of us possess –
holding onto things
which are no longer
part of our lives.

Yet, there's a comfort
knowing the
paraphernalia is up there
just in case.
Just in case we decide
to use those old
Christmas decorations one day.

Just in case we need a tent
even though it's been a decade
since we even thought of camping.
Just in case
some of those old outdated
computer cords might come in handy.

When we move again,
there will be no attic to store
all those hangers-on.
It will have to be dealt with.
Most, if not all, discarded.
Thrown away. Permanently erased.

I wonder how often we retain
antiquated ideas and emotional baggage
somewhere in the attic of our mind?
Keeping them there
even though we no longer use them
or need them.
But stored nevertheless,
just in case.

You Will Be OK

When the ground
swallows you whole
and you no longer
see the light –
take a breath,
and then another.
You will be alright.

If you're at
the bottom –
the depths
of your despair.
Realize you're
not the first.
Many have
visited there.

Perhaps you choose
to remain in bed
and stay there
throughout the day.
Lay in your sorrow.
Get up tomorrow.
You will be ok.

Make today a woodland hike.
Take a walk in the rain.
See the seasons
for what they are –
earthly therapy
for your pain.

Autumn says goodbye.
Winter's introspection.
Spring brings forth renewal.
Summer's warm reception.

Darkness is periodic.
Surely comes the day.
Nature assures
things do get better.
You will be ok.

Camping Our Way to Reno

Off on our new adventure
in my parent's Layton trailer –
and me, a brooding sixteen.
Too old to continue
being the child that I'd been.
Too young to break
my family's loving heart.

Found a place to set up camp
and hold up for the night.
A place among the Ponderosa pine.
Enough off the road to let nature speak.
And listen to the quiet.

I took my little notebook
and sat by the edge of the creek.
Time of change. Time of growth.
Time to ponder the mystique.
I scribbled my thoughts on paper.
Composed a little poem.
There was not much for me
to enjoy once in Reno.
Would have rather been home.

Reno would yield a few adventures
which couldn't have been foreseen.
The discovery of my Crooks cigars
found at the bottom of my magazines.
How could I tell them they were my defense
from peer pressure of other teens –
They'd smoke their marijuana
while I'd smoke a stogy fraternally.

I took my lumps of parental concern.
Endured all the smoking warnings
and the punishment to fit the crime.
It was my last real family vacation with them.
I was yearning to be free.

(That poem which I wrote then, originally published in my
first book, *Colors of My Within*, is presented on page 131)

Colors of Joy

All in my memory –
Colors of my joy.
Variety of ecstasy.
Delight I will deploy.

Mesmerize my mortal mind.
Enslave my loving heart.
Sweep me off my feet again.
Seduce me in the dark.

Captivate my very soul.
Bewitch me with your charm.
Intrigue me; infatuate –
Awaken me with your warm.

My joy has many colors.
Each a precious gem.
Pearls of my pleasure.
A gratifying friend.

Some are soft and delicate.
Some are large and loud.
Some in the quiet of the night.
Some like a thundercloud.

It's delivered in many ways.
All sorts of shapes and sizes.
Times when it's predictable.
And sometimes simply surprises.

There is always disappointment.
Trouble and dismay.
But when joy decides to come around
it always makes my day.

Ginger

Her name was Virginia,
but everyone called her Ginger.
Mother's younger sister, my aunt.
Back when I was a kid,
before the watermelon in
her stomach turned into cousin Sandy,
Ginger would take me places.
A tryout to see what
this "child stuff" was all about.
Once was to a movie where we
watched Disney's *The Shaggy Dog*.
Another time shopping in downtown Seattle.
The experience I remember most
was going to some kind of fair
where I had my eye on a large red helium balloon,
which she bought for me.
The balloon man tied the string
around my wrist so I wouldn't lose it.
I had it in my head that
only babies had balloons tied on
and big kids held their strings.
So, after a half an hour of my
incessant whining, Ginger succumbed.
I held the balloon the entire time
and was looking forward to taking it home,
tying a small basket to it and
playing *Around the World in 80 Days*.
But just as I was getting into the car to go home,
the string slipped from my fingers
and the balloon began to rise, escaping my grasp.
It was gone. I watched it with tears
as it journeyed into the sky,
dancing about in the wind as if happy to be free.
Ginger did not buy me another one.
My lesson to learn.

Ginger passed away at 84.
I think of her now as that balloon –
rising to the heavens,
free from all earthly restraints.
She was a special aunt to me,
always close because of those
precious childhood bonding times.
If I had my way, though,
she would still be here,
tethered to me with a string around my wrist,
tied tight with a strong knot –
so I would never have to let her go.

Public Meeting

Thank you for all who chose to be here today.
Sorry if we are starting a little late, but we had
only 20 minutes to set up nine tripods to display
large panels of useless and irrelevant information.
Even the head of our Engineering Department
had trouble figuring those darn things out.
A special thanks to Frank Gardner who found
all those hymnals we could place under
the projector so our Powerpoint presentation
could be somewhat viewable on the screen.

Did everyone here get a comment card?
I know we'll be discussing some controversial
issues today and this is the method your opinions
will be heard. So, fill them out while
writing uncomfortably using your lap.
We'll gather them all at the end of the meeting
and type them on one big comment sheet.
Then we'll forward the sheet to our superiors
and the City Council who will probably ignore it
and we'll do what we intend to anyway.
This way, you'll feel a part of the process.

Now I know a lot of you would love to speak,
but first we have a canned 30 minute briefing
which will not only bore you to tears but will
outline some of our unsubstantial assumptions
that we have based our decision-making upon.
Remember, as community leaders, it is
our job to tell you what you need,
certainly not the other way around.
We will then open the floor to public comment
for whatever time remaining allows.

So, let's begin this awkward and ineffective
attempt at fairness and democracy
as we tell you what will be happening
right in your neighborhood. Thanks again
for paying your taxes and our salaries
and letting us provide the most inept,
unfair and disregardful service possible.

Warped Wisdom

Construct a simple sentence
with only averse verbs.
Cook like a gourmet chef
and use no healthy herbs.
Don't try to look for trouble
until you are disturbed.
Spin a yarn, use your charm,
separate from the herd.
You can't repair a rainbow
or pull wool from a bird.
Won't get where you're going
if your route has been deferred.
Wisdom comes from inner truth
not from a bunch of nerds.
The meaning of life is never known
when the question is so absurd.

Freedom

It was the early 70's and peace, love, dove was in full swing. I, along with my sidekick, were to interview Woodstock icon Richie Havens after his Kennedy Pavilion concert.

During his performance, he did an extended and inspired version of his song *Freedom* which had ignited fans afire at Woodstock and brought the crowd to their feet at Kennedy. I remember him saying to the crowd, *"I grew up believing in truth, justice and the American way,"* obviously referring to the opening sequence of the '50's Superman television series. *"But then,"* he said, *"I had always thought truth and justice WERE the American way."*

We waited in the men's locker room for 45 minutes after the concert and Richie emerged. No agents. No sycophants. Just this slight and sincere man – exhausted from a two-hour performance – talking to two seventeen-year-olds like they were family. He, the sage. The wise old uncle. We talked about his early years in Greenwich Village, sharing the stage with Dylan and Joni Mitchell. We learned about his life and what got him up in the morning, spreading the word of peace as his mission, his calling.

I remember hitting Dick's Drive-in on the way home – a late night burger and fries – Wayne and I flying high on this personal trip we had shared with one of our culture's greatest icons. It was if we somehow became a part of his whole life adventure when we all had said goodbye and hugged as brothers.

On the car ride back to Cheney, we both repeated the same phrase to each other as if it were conversation – *Richie Fuckin' Havens! Richie Fuckin' Havens! Richie Fuckin' Havens!*

Honest Abe

He'd be a turnin' in his grave –
Honest Abe.
At least that's what we're taught.
A saint on the penny
and five dollar bill.
Freedom and equality sought.

I'm sure he fought formidable foes –
precarious undertows of political currents.
His honesty was more than a line,
building faith and trust among
his growing party of constituents.

How different it is today for
candidates to follow those steps.
Integrity lost in a spacious wasteland.
Deceit under the carpet swept.
We need another Honest Abe
not a closer off the bench –
pitching us curve balls and sliders
striking out our virtue
and common sense.

Could there be another
Honest Abe?
That really is the question.
Caught in a compromising position?
Somewhere a past transgression?

We would make a liar
out of Honest Abe.
Diminish his truth to rubble.
Today's political arena,
a stench of pigsty.
With wrestlers in the muddle.

Bit of a Pickle

Heard from a Nigerian Prince today –
of all people – via email, believe it or not.
He must have done extensive research
to learn – as a trustworthy individual –
I am honest as the day is long and
would never betray his confidence.

He's in a bit of a pickle
and can't access his rightful share
of oil money – millions of dollars
due to him and his royal family.
He needs to transfer the funds
into United States dollars and
an American bank account
where the assets can be fairly dispersed.

A reasonable proposition.
Especially when he offered me,
a lowly poet, a third of all the money.
An outrageous payment for
letting this penniless prince
claim back his legitimate fortune
via my personal bank account.
I offered to do it for a quarter of it,
but he insisted I deserved the full reward.

I believe in helping people
who cannot help themselves.
But there had to be a more
needy person who could benefit
from this tremendous generosity.
So, with great nuance and subtlety
I composed my courteous refusal.

Then, before I sent it, my decision swiveled.
Someone might think this proposal a hoax.
It could fall into the wrong hands.
It's up to me to right this wrong –
bring prosperity back to
the philanthropic prince once again.

He said he needed only $5000 to put
all the money transfers in motion.
Where would a poor poet get $5000 anyway?
So, I sent him my well-written refusal
and wished him a fond farewell.

Obviously, his research
was not as comprehensive
as I originally believed.

Love

Love is more than infatuation.
Not that it's not a part of it.
But love is the thing that sticks around
when another has drama.
Love is poise that doesn't perish.
A carafe of caring ready to pour –
to sip, to soothe, to smooth
out the rough edges of the day.
Love assures. Love endures.
It's the greatest gift we humans have,
sharing love with someone else.
The foundation of any real relationship.
It doesn't have to be flowery
or syrupy sweet.
It just has to come from the heart.
That's where it lives.
How it forgives.
Remains when all else departs.

Cabbages and Kings

Perhaps it was the walrus
who conjured up the stew.
His love for oysters, vast.
More than anyone ever knew.

"Better with a side of slaw"
said the carpenter, quite convincing.
A point he would always hammer down,
especially if he'd been drinking.

Feeding the magnate of the crown
takes courage with such cuisine.
*"Let's first taste the flavorful food
to assure it's fit for a king."*

So, each began to sample the treat –
just a little would not be wrong.
Soon, cabbage was in short supply
and crustaceans were good as gone.

Assuming it warranted a royal feast
may have been quite priggish.
But to share a fare that wasn't there
was completely beyond shellfish.

News from the Raven Haven

It's been a cool July.
Not that I'm complaining.
But the garden is.
Fourth of July tomatoes,
still green on the vine
twelve days later.
They need more heat to ripen.

Tom turkey visits daily.
Leaves feathers for Donna
outside her office window.
He rests there, seeing his reflection,
admiring his beautiful beard.
Molts as if it were late summer.

Time to trim the lavender.
And deadhead the roses.
Our black-eyed susans
are taller than I remember.
And the hydrangeas are
finally flowering this year.

Tuffy's eye is clearing up.
Thor's still sneezin'.
An old folks' home for felines.
Eagerly eating morning grass,
only to puke it up later.

Two children fell from
their raft into the river,
fortunately rescued by their father.
The prompt emergency rescue crew
gave the gathering crowd a thumbs up.

It wasn't a mass murder.
Or a bombing. Or a coup.
But it was a little excitement
in our corner of the world.
Where discussing politics and religion
is not nearly as important as
turkey feathers and ripe tomatoes.

Something's Brewing

I remember 1968. Vietnam raged.
Johnson signed the Civil Rights Act.
Martin Luther King assassinated.
Patchouli incense burned in the air.
Fervor of furor everywhere.
Not a time of nonchalance.
Protest and dissent.
Youth culture found a voice.

Drafted at eighteen.
No vote 'til twenty-one.
Nixon elected in November.
Farewell to our favorite sons.
You could smell it in the air.
Feel it in your bones.
Change was in the wind again.
Couldn't be postponed.

Something's brewing now.
Like 1968.
Jet streams new direction.
Pendulum of fate.
Transformation for mankind?
Or blind leading the blind?
History doesn't repeat itself,
but it does often rhyme.

Something's brewing.

Masked Marauders

They come for bounty
in the dark of night,
concealed in shadows,
hidden from sight.

Capriciously choosing
their plunder and prey.
Unwelcome, they enter.
Unwanted, they stay.

An interlude of malice –
these nocturnal pirates.
Mercenaries of opulence
now public, once private.

They steal the dreams,
the trust, the tears.
Hijack the tranquility,
replace it with fear.

Then as sun rises,
suddenly they disappear.
Off swashbuckling another realm,
an otherworldly sphere.

Did the marauders grace mercy?
Quite the opposite of that.
Abducting hours of precious slumber
from its native habitat.

Beam Me Up

Speeding through stars
at meteoric warp speed –
makes even the present
one big blur.

No stopping to enjoy the scenery.
No picnic on Pluto.
Racing with Auriga the Charioteer.
Heading for another hemisphere.

I lament my youthful earthen existence
when days were so long I was bored.
Today, there's never enough time.
Too busy. Constantly moving forward.

That's the thing about aging.
Moments become more precious
because they're much more fleeting.
Memories dispel in the chemtrails.

There will come a time
when my fountain of youth
no longer produces cascading water
with its restorative resource.

I hope I'll be in range
of the mothership.
Maneuver my molecules.
And beam me up. Beam me up.

Florida Euphoria

His dream girl lived in Florida.
But they had only talked online.
A month had past – seemed to last.
Saw her for real at Christmas time.
Long distance relationship. 3000 miles apart.

Amazing what a guy will do
involving matters of the heart.
His cronies tried to warn him,
but he'd hear none of that.
It was meant to be, she lived by the sea.
Heard their wisdom as a bunch of flack.

The dream became reality.
A holiday in the Florida sun.
Succulent seafood at a beach café.
Was like a lottery he had won.

The first visit ended way too soon.
Plans were made for another.
A few weeks later he was off again
to see his far away lover.

This time however, it was different.
The bloom was off the rose.
She was hoping for permanence.
Hinting he propose.

He wanted his cake and eat it too.
That's the way the story goes.
Grass is always greener
on the other side it grows.

Harvest Adieu

Our tomato bounty has
been abundant this year.
A welcome, fresh addition
to our dining table.
Alas, as autumn emerges,
the remainder on the vine
ripen slower or not at all,
leaving us green tomatoes
to fry up or store
with hope some eventually ripen.
It seems so temporary –
this growing and harvesting process.
The lifespan of living, then dying,
over a course of only a few months.
When we no longer have our
private stock of tomato sauce,
processed, frozen and preserved
for a hearty winter meal –
we'll be forced to purchase
store-bought brands,
mass produced in hot houses
or on Mexican farms.
Tasteless compared
to ones grown on our own soil.
Always a sad and yet,
bittersweet goodbye.
But a fleeting summer love affair
we'll begin again in spring.

Chinook

She blows in
from the southwest
like a warm embrace –
thawing the cool
apple-crisp miasma
with her sultry breath.
Frosty chills
rapidly melt away –
propelled by her
feverish desire.

Rhymes with Orange

It was said
in something I read
that nothing rhymes with orange.
Perhaps it's true
but it's a bit of a rue
when it sounds so much like porridge.
Perhaps they're not brother or sister
or even mom or dad –
at least a second cousin
with a conviction of Galahad.
Let the hijinks begin and
the sorta rhymes flourish.
Squeeze the fruit to make it rhyme
and let the nectar nourish.
You can't grow an orange
in Anchorage –
yet acknowledge
it could come from storage.
Nothing should ever discourage
a fruitful word search forage.
You might find it an arduous task
but please don't have a hemorrhage.
An orange when juiced
in a rhyming glass
makes a delicious beverage.

Giving Up Smoking

My father had a running joke –
that he was an expert at
giving up smoking –
he had done it dozens of times.
But that afternoon in the car
was no laughing matter.
He recently began smoking again. Winstons.
My mother was not pleased.
News reports talked about a
direct link to cigarettes and cancer.
She knew it wasn't good for him.
Witnessing the discussion
from the back seat, I knew
the debate was getting serious.
They had married young, 18 and 19,
and were in the middle of
raising a family.
She wasn't afraid to tell him
what was on her mind.
He told her to lay off.
Mind her own business.
She began to cry. Weep.
He picked an unfortunate time
to light up a cigarette,
taking the first puff to calm his nerves,
settle things down.
A moment to gather his thoughts.
At first, I thought she had slapped him.
Then I saw the lit cigarette
fly out of his mouth and onto
the '56 Plymouth Belvedere's floor.
"You're killing our family!" she sobbed.
My mother had her hands over her eyes.
I screamed, *"Mommy, are you all right?"*
Dad yelled, *"You kids shut up!"*
Besides sounds of muffled whimpering,
it was quiet the rest of the drive home.
Dad never told the joke about
giving up smoking again.

That day, he quit for good.

An Endless Summer Day

When I was young,
summer days seemed to last forever.
September, so many miles away.
Christmas – an infinity.

I yearned to be older.
The adult world seemed
so much more fun.
One can drive.
Eat what one wants.
Go to bed much later.

As each year passed, though,
time accelerated.
No longer did one day
feel like it would never end.
Now, in my '60's
each day simply blurs by
like looking through a window on a train.

I want off this rapid railroad.
Let me depart at the next depot,
so I can once again get
those eternal summer days back.
But it's not slowing down.
Still getting a little faster every day.

If I had known it would be like this,
I may have not aspired to getting older.
Seems it's an unfair trade off,
swapping youth for privilege –
paying for it in the only currency
we really have. Time.

Now, I can only think back and remember
when 24 hours in summer
was like an all-day jawbreaker,
accepting the challenge to make it last.
Then placing it on one's bedside table
until tomorrow.

Nine Lives

Cats, they say, have nine lives.
Nine chances to cheat death
before the inevitable.
Perhaps the same applies to all of us.
But what if sometimes
you don't get to know it's over?

When the Suzuki Samuri was broadsided
in the intersection of Indiana and Monroe,
slamming the car 20 feet in the air
and landing, like a cat, upright,
yards away from the impact,
with all the windshield glass gone
leaving tiny remnants in my eyes –
I should have been dead.
I shouldn't have been able to
locate my brick of a phone
and call my wife to tell her
there had been an accident,
but I was ok.
Was I, really?
Or were there two dimensions
where I was alive no longer in one
and picking glass out of my eyes
in the other?
The transition is simultaneous.
It's very hard to tell the difference
between one's previous reality
and the reality you have fallen into.
Each has the same cast of players.
The past remains the same.
It's the future that is different
because you are now in a world
you wouldn't have been, otherwise.

My lives are diminishing.
I certainly have used up more than a few.
Having already travelled to
my share of alternative dimensions,
each time leaving behind
the sadness of my departure.
Gaining a new world of hope and promise
in the reality I'm living in today.

In a Drawer

My grandmother
kept her nice clothes
in a drawer, many
still in the original package.
Gifts from birthdays and Mother's Day.
Too nice to wear.
It would drive my mother wild,
seeing grandma
in old plaid working dresses
and tattered, mended sweaters.
"You would look so nice
in that pretty peach blouse
I gave you last year."
Grandma smiled,
belting out her cackling laugh,
"So lovely," she said.
"for a special occasion."
She was comfortable
in her old worn clothes.
Like old friends by her side
as she gathered eggs every morning.
As a kid, I don't remember
caring about what grandma wore.
I just knew she was always
loving, warm and cheerful.
Making me a cup of children's tea
whenever I came to visit.
My mother finally began buying her
other things than clothes
since they continued to lay waiting,
in her drawer, for that fancy time when
she felt she deserved to wear them.

Holidaze

It's almost upon us –
that period from
Thanksgiving through
New Years.
The holidaze.
Got my big bag
of tangerines already,
but I'm no better prepared.
Figuring out gifts –
a turbid affair.
Battling store crowds.
Decorations. Feasts.
Family togetherness
with inlaws and outlaws.
If only I could go off on a tangent
and arrive back January second
with tales of terns
sharing solace by the sea.
But it's the holidaze,
so, get ready.
Have a hot buttered rum
or a tasty Tom and Jerry.
Embrace Rudolph's red nose.
And Santa's jelly belly.
I want to be pleasant.
Compassionate. Kind.
But if you take that last piece of pie,
you're clearly out of your mind.

Pig Leather

By the age of eleven
I needed dress shoes for church and school.
My memory recalls It was
with more than some angst
I accompanied my mother to the shoe store.
She was tired of seeing my nice shoes
always scuffed, scraped, looking dogged.
Dad would polish them occasionally,
but I would demolish the shine much faster.

We looked for shoes on the bargain rack
because paying full price just wasn't done.
She would pick out the choices
and the shoe salesman would do the fitting.
Many of the shoes that were on sale
hadn't been sold for a reason.
They might have been ugly.
Old fashioned. Impractical. Strange.

The right choice meant I would slip
through unnoticed. Camouflaged.
Part of the commonplace crowd.
The wrong choice meant awkwardness.
Teasing. Torture. Taunting
Mocking and harassment.
Today was the day I was getting
a new pair of shoes, like it or not.
Then, after the third pair of shoes
I was certain would put me in category two,
the salesman went into the back room
and emerged with suede oxfords.

They fit beautifully. My mother said,
"At least he won't have to polish them."
All I cared about was I had seen
other kids with similar shoes
and they were not in the geek, freak,
dolt, goon, buffoon league. For once,
I had shoes I could be proud of.
On the way home, I asked her what suede was.
She said, with certainty, *"pig leather"*.

Extravagance

As a kid, I never knew money was tight.
We had food on the table, mostly from our farm.
Produce from our garden.
Eggs from our chickens.
Beef, pork and lamb we raised ourselves.
However, I did learn
many things were *extravagant* –
a big word for a seven year old.

Going out for dinner
unless a *very* special occasion:
Extravagant.
Brand name tennis shoes
instead of imported knock-offs:
Extravagant.
A visit to the vet for any of our pets:
Extravagant.
If something was broken,
one got the part and fixed it.
Repairmen were *extravagant.*
I had a passbook savings account –
which could never be spent
on something *extravagant.*
It was too difficult to save money
to blow it on something superficial.

I think about what might be
considered *extravagant* today.
Smart phones with 128 gigabytes?
Premium cable services like HBO?
A home Kegerator for beer on tap?
Things have changed since I was young.
Certainly, so has our extravagance.
I wonder if kids still wear
older sibling hand-me-downs?
Or are forced to play the eldest's cornet?
Perhaps the rising tide of our standard of living
has altered the meaning of extravagance itself.

I, for one, wish that some of those values
had never disappeared.

Perspective

Children starving in India.
Adults, too. But they don't get the press.
Or as many donations as a crying child.
Usually we wait for a disaster to happen
before we open our hearts and pocketbooks.

Floods in China and Peru.
Heavy snowfall in Afghanistan.
Landslides in the Congo.
Dengue Fever in Sri Lanka.
Earthquakes in Mexico.
Deluge in Columbia.
Mudslides in Sierra Leone.
Monsoon rains affecting 41 million people
In India, Bangladesh and Nepal –
leaving over twelve hundred dead
and sprouting more than 2,000 relief camps.

Hurricanes. Tornados.
Tsunamis. Volcanos.
Horrible natural disasters causing
devastating human consequences.
We can't do anything to stop
Mother Earth's unruly nature.
All we can do is offer relief
for the survivors.
And believe
some of those dollars will do some good.

Next time you're upset
because you have a bad day.
Or if something doesn't go your way,
reflect upon how things could be –
No food; shelter; water; hope.
It's all a matter of perspective.

Just My Age

I'm at that stage
of my current age
when there's more
to see backward
than ahead.

Check the gauge,
turn the page.
I'd still rather
look forward
instead.

Can't live life
in the rear view.
Must cross
new bridges
as they come.

A lot of living
left to do.
Love and laughter –
my riches.
Yarn that I have spun.

The past –
a wealth of reminisce.
Future days, so precious.
Time I simply cannot miss
before it sifts to stardust.

Pardon me if I sip my tea
and linger at sunsets longer.
It's just my age,
I'm more engaged
to savor moments stronger.

Cotton Candy

It was fascinating watching the operator
pour from a five pound bag of sugar
into a swirling aluminum machine –
spinning granular sweetness into a
featherweight magical confection.
She would take a long, slender paper cone
and roll it around inside the circular tub,
gathering the goodness until
it looked like a small pink tree in fairyland.
Then it was mine to imbibe,
still warm from its creation.
It was a scene commonplace in my youth
at store grand openings, county fairs
and other celebrations.
But now, cotton candy comes pre-made –
complete with a sanitary plastic bag
around the whole tasty treat.
I wonder if it's just less expensive
and more efficient
to make and sell it that way.
Or perhaps it was the dental association
promoting a polemic campaign
that simply put live operators
completely out of business.

Sotto Mare

Eating luscious seafood –
me, ordained with a bib.
I'm not the neatest eater.
"I won't spill" would be a fib.
Best Cioppino in San Francisco.
At least that's what they say.
A hike up the hill to find it.
Definitely worth the wait.
Docile sea creatures swimming
in an Italian tomato sauce.
Mussels, shrimp, scallops and ample crab.
A delicious shellfish holocaust.
Enjoy the sourdough, but save room
for that scrumptious seafood stew.
The serving portion is so large
it can easily be enjoyed by two.

Pollyanna

Show me another video
with frolicking kittens.
Puppies playing.
Or billy goats
on teeter totters.
I don't personally enjoy
seeking out these things
on this Internet forum,
but they are blissfully benign.
They are not about hate.
Or prejudice. Or politics.
If I wanted your opinion
I would have asked for it.
The social network has become
polluted with unpleasantness.
It's become a medium
for every crackpot to
ram their personal agenda
into the entire Facebook brood.
Now they are posting live –
murdering innocents for
five minutes of fleeting fame.
I want birthdays.
Flower gardens.
Vacations. Exotic locations.
Tell me how your Doctor visit went.
Show me photos of your grandchildren.
Or when you were a grandchild
on throwback Thursday.
I don't care who you voted for,
your dating drama
or why your religion is the only one.

Let's connect –
all of us –
embracing the human condition.
We all have so much more in common
than the trifles that set us apart.

The Kissing Disease

We began dating in autumn
and went to the Sadie Hawkins dance
at your invitation. We walked
each other to class, holding hands.
You sewed me a red, white and blue
patterned shirt for Christmas and gifted
a package of forbidden rum-soaked,
wine-dipped cigars.

You came from a large Catholic family
and your mother hated me – the
Methodist boyfriend – the minute
she met me. Maybe even before.
No matter how nice or polite I was.
Even though I had to face the scowl
at the door, it never deterred me
from coming over.

I managed the high school
radio station and lifeguarded
at the local pool. You worked part time
as an assistant for my dentist,
ironically enough. We talked about
the future. College. Dreaming with
abandon how our lives would intertwine.

Then, I caught mononucleosis,
the kissing disease.

My spleen hurt. Two weeks of bed rest.
Then school only and afternoon naps.
Even though we talked on the phone,
I could feel you fading, pulling away.
We didn't kiss for two months
and when we did, it felt different.
You said it was over – yet
still went to the senior prom with me.
And bought me a beautiful sweater.

Mono had made me weak,
sucking out my stamina.
The kissing disease left me unemployed
with an abandoned relationship.
I heard you were dating an older guy
during the summer. Thirty-two,
if I recall.

I wonder what your mother thought of him?

Coloring Outside the Lines

When I was young I got in trouble
coloring outside the lines.
It didn't seem important then
for art to be refined.
There are far worse things
more deserving of a crime.
Kept it loose,
endured abuse of
what perfectionists' define.

Today, there's no crayolas.
The metaphor manifests.
Thinking outside the box
seems much easier to digest.
No longer a problem child
who failed the coloring test.
It's desirable now
to simply know how
to be unorthodox by request.

I'm thankful I see things differently –
it keeps solutions fresh.
Abandon rules, seed the clouds,
create new ways for success.
Don't seclude that little soul who
won't conform or be defined.
Might just be the next Einstein who
colors outside the lines.

Flower Child

Her name was Azalea.
Middle name, Dahlia.
Born to blossom and thrive.
She could put roots down anywhere.
Instinctively survive.

Didn't care about money.
Sold pint jars of honey.
Earned enough coin to get by.
Peace and love, her mission.
Ambition never applied.

What became of such gentle souls –
the friends of earth and sky?
Grew like weeds during Aquarius.
Now in short supply.

I miss the carefree flower child.
Why couldn't she sustain?
The world became a different place.
Her petals down the drain.

Give a flower to a stranger.
A smile to passersby.
We need more gentle natures
and less who polarize.

Knack of Lacking

Pencil with warn eraser.
Deflated basketball.
Flashlight without batteries
won't shine bright at all.
Diet without discipline.
Dog without a bone.
Painter with no brush.
A wallet left at home.
Thunder without lightning.
Pepper without salt.
Blame without reason –
usually no one's fault.
Singer with no voice.
Writer with no words.
Never can reach first place
if you always come in third.
Storm with no shelter.
Sleep without dreams.
Forgotten memories
swept away downstream.
Clay without a sculptor.
Project without a plan.
Two without a tango.
Can't without a can.
Up when there's no down.
Back without a forth.
Map with wrong directions.
South without a North.
Plus with no minus.
Push without a shove.
Life with no living
when it doesn't come with love.

A Novel Approach

The written word, a little blurb –
grows tall into a book.
The book then
gains a life of its own –
giving far more time
than it took.
Peruse your library
for your next refresher.
Grapes of Wrath, a fruitful find,
The Da Vinci Code, a treasure.
Ulysses stands tall against the wall,
The Fountainhead
weighs a man's measure.
A Brave New World,
explores utopia.
Call of the Wild
an adventure.
On the Road is hard to beat,
The Sound and the Fury –
southern splendor.
Persnickety readers
reject *Portnoy's Complaint*
while *Tropic of Cancer*
can be wherever.
Find the novel that fits
The Age of Innocence
or stretch your *Guilty Pleasures.*
It's not just *The World According to Garp*
or *Stranger in a Strange Land.*
A few lines read and you are
Gone with the Wind.
Through the Looking Glass – a wonderland.

Medium Well

I sometimes think about
the adventure that awaits us
as we pass through middle age
and fall into
whatever they call it after that.
Old age doesn't seem right.
Not ready for the rocking chair, yet.
Perhaps, like a great steak,
we'll be prepared
medium well.
Too seasoned to be rare.
Too tender to be well done.

If we both can
keep the scourge of
disease and disability at bay,
we'll have time to enjoy
our life medium well.
Take long walks together.
Talk. Laugh. Cry.
Watch our wrinkles get wrinkles.
Knowing
we're not going to be
a trade-in for a newer model.
We're already both broken in –
with softer corners
and a familiar fit.

Sure, we'll have our aches and pains.
Every birthday, more arthritis.
Let's not fear the next step
of life's incredible journey.
As long as we're together
we can enjoy the world
through each other's eyes
and savor the softness of our love
through each other's hearts.

I'll take my sojourn
into the age of medium well
holding hands with you.

Selling like Hot Cakes

A little flour, a little egg,
A perfect pancake
I can make.
A little chocolate
in the swirl
Let's give that tasty cake
a whirl.
Ready now to
sell my wares -
Butter and syrup,
the perfect pair.

*Will you buy
my lovely cakes?*
A delicious breakfast
they will make.
*Someone else is
selling some?
Better than mine?
Even more fun?*

So they bought from them instead
and it made me sad –
They were offering pancakes
in moire and plaid.

Puyallup Fair

Nearly every year of my childhood,
my family would visit the Puyallup Fair.
Largest annual exposition in Washington State.
I remember happily winning a pound of bacon
at a carny booth.
Then realizing I had to carry it around the
remainder of the day.
The US Forest Service had a larger than life
animated Smokey the Bear, saying
"Only you can prevent forest fires"
at the touch of a button.

One year, the Markwick family met us there
and I palled around with cousin Danny,
one year older.
As young teens, we went right to the amusements
and began carefully considered what rides
we'd spend our limited funds on,
Danny's eye caught the attention of a girl
just as she was getting on the roller coaster.
It was the first time I ever witnessed
that magic moment of instant connection.
He was immediately crazy about her.
By the look on her face, the feeling was mutual.
Her car, climbing the first hill, rolled out of sight.
"We'll wait until her ride is over –
and I'll take her again!"

Danny certainly wasn't shy.
"So, this is how this meeting girls thing works,"
I thought to myself.
But then Diane, the oldest, came up to us in a huff
and explained brother Donald was in a fight
and Danny needed to come help. Now! So, he left.
He said he'd be back. When she got off the ride,
I was to keep her here until he returned.
"OK," I said. A solemn vow.

So, I watched the roller coaster go up and
down its hilly tracks. *What should I say to her?*
Explain I'm the cousin of the guy who
caught her eye? Would she even remember?
I didn't want to let Danny down.

But this was a predicament! The coaster ride
was over and a mass of humanity rushed out
the exit. *Where is she? What did she look like
again?* I just had the one glance.

I watched people come and go for fifteen min-
utes and couldn't locate her face in the crowd.
Danny finally made it back –
amply disappointed.
We spent another hour or two
searching for her to no avail.
Never did go on any rides.

Met up with my Mom, Dad and sister
at the pre-discussed time and place –
the Fischer Flour Mill booth, where my father
promptly ordered four hot raspberry scones,
one of our longtime family fair traditions.

It was a sweet ending to an adventurous day,
where I learned a lot more about life and love
than preventing forest fires.

The Little Tramp

There's something romantic
about the little tramp –
the Charlie Chaplin kind.
Colorful cloth bindle,
tied to the end of a hobo stick.
All worldly possessions
thrust over the shoulder –
a homeless vagabond
wandering off to the
next big adventure –
hopping a freight train
west to new frontiers.

Where are those ragamuffins now?
Do they still walk the tracks
looking for better luck elsewhere?
Or have they transformed
into beggars with cardboard signs?
Street people cluttering
downtown sidewalks,
compelled to live
off the kindness of others,
with a grudge against
a good days' work and the
satisfaction of self-sufficiency.

I miss the time of the little tramp –
my innocence of the sadder,
pathetic parts of humanity –
and perhaps the fantasy
that vagrants will bounce back
from their hard luck story
as productive members of society again.

People once laughed at the
quirky little tramp –
part clown, part pitied, part pluck.
Today, they are laughing no longer.

The Bitterroot

There are days when the
Bitterroot foothills are visible
and days when they simply
disappear in cloud cover.
It's been our way
to document the seasons –
waiting until all the snow
melts from its caps
before planting in late spring.
These broad shoulders to the East
cradle our valley view
and look back at us like gods –
blessing the mature maples
and the horse pasture
in all its green gallant glory.

Soon, our view of this treasure
will be blocked out by *"progress"* –
entry level homes four feet apart.
Destroying the pasture
and those magnificent maples
with asphalt and cement –
our private innocence replaced
with cookie-cutter cottages.

We will just have to pretend
the foothills are obscured by fog,
as will our hearts,
when our view is blocked forever.

Escape

Clicked her ruby slippers
wanting to go home.
Counted sheep to go to sleep
jumping the fence alone.
Dreamt of reincarnation,
wishing it was true.
Returned as a sacred cow –
eating steak taboo.
Searched for life's answers, hoping
escape might just be one.
Unfortunately, it's the real world.
Nowhere else to run.

No Place Like Oz

Off to see the wizard.
Escape. Adventure.
Grass is always greener,
especially in Oz.
Exit from the real world,
where munchkins are dwarfs
plagued by a genetic
or medical condition.

Off to see the wizard.
Cavorting with
familiar strangers.
High drama to
get back home
and flee this world
of fantasy.

Kill the witch.
End the scourge.
Something the
wizard couldn't even do.
Flies away alone in a big balloon.
Can't come back because
he doesn't know how it works.

Ruby slippers from
the first witch she killed.
Her ticket home all along.
Back in bed.
Waking from a bad dream.
There's no place like home.
And no place like Oz, either.

Small Miracles

Born to a mother
whose inverted nipples
didn't allow breastfeeding.
Rejecting formula, producing
homemade cottage cheese.
Finally adjusted to cow's milk.
Small miracle.

At four, he told his Mom
his stomach hurt,
especially when he ran
or played on the swingset.
During hernia surgery,
doctor boasted the
belly button was saved.
Another small miracle.

At thirty-three, an appendectomy.
Waking up on the surgical table,
aspirating acid into lungs,
coughing, choking,
complicating the procedure,
shocking the anesthesiologist.
Small miracle he could
breathe normally again.

At fifty, he complained
of numbness in his feet
and the sensation of
a girdle around his waist.
Tested for heavy metal poisoning
and vitamin deficiencies with
a diagnosis six months later
of multiple sclerosis.
Daily copaxone injections –
a *small miracle* for
delaying the progression.

A heart attack at fifty-seven.
Rushed to the hospital
with complete blockage
of a main artery.
Sixty percent chance of survival
meant a forty percent chance of death.
Small miracle the on-call surgeon
placed the metal stent successfully.

Verbal difficulties at sixty-three
during poetry workshop.
Small blood clot lodged in brain,
cause of the startling stroke.
Drove himself home,
not seeking medical attention
until the following day.
Small miracle he survived.

Small miracle
there's such a thing
as *small miracles* –
especially as
they increasingly grow larger.
And continue
to keep him alive.

Back Porch

I long for a summer's eve
on the back porch
In shirt sleeves –
embracing a star-lit sky.

A cold beer.
Chicken on the grill.
Relaxing between turnings.
Gentle summer breeze
cooling me to comfortable.

Our back porch
gives solace.
A cozy chair
with time to spare.
Privacy. Peace.

I like it best with you.
Our conversations
of hopes and dreams –
born on the back porch
with a cool gin and tonic.

Our getaway
from the world's noise.
Shangrila for the two of us.
We don't have to travel far
to love our local wanderlust.

It's a sad day
when it's all put away.
Protected from winter's breath.
Come spring
back porch begins again –
Tranquil place of rest.

Gratitude

My hope is to always have
more blessings than regrets.
More things on course.
Raincoat my remorse.
To give more than I get.
I'm thankful for the simple things -
Awakening to a new day.
Appreciating the love around me.
Even breathing, by the way.
I don't take my health for granted.
Or others who share my soul.
Life is but a one way journey.
Bridges with an occasional toll.

Geometry

I turned in the right answer
but teacher was quite aloof.
"We need to see your work," she said.
"We need to see your proof."

"Shape, size – position and properties
play a roll in your execution.
Show me how you came upon
the conclusion of your solution."

"I looked at planes and angles –
the lines, curves and points.
For me, it was complete chaos.
A tangent with no joint."

The path of two parallel lines
will never meet their maker.
I simply skipped the wearisome task
and copied off Debra's paper.

Learning from Regrets

I regret biting Tommy Rowan's finger in first grade.
I told him to put his finger in my mouth. He did.
So, I bit him. Drew blood.
I'm in trouble?
He's the one who put his finger in my mouth!

I hadn't ever done anything like that before.
Or since.
I obviously learned, at six years old,
that particular behavior was unacceptable.
I don't regret learning that lesson.
But I did feel bad for Tommy.
His bleeding finger wrapped in tissue,
fighting his way through tears, shuffling
down the hallway to the school nurse.
I regret causing him pain.
I regret instigating the commotion,
interrupting regular classroom activities.

Three decades later, Thomas Rowan's
brilliant dissertation – the Functional
Stability Analysis of Numerical Algorithms –
helped him earn a Doctorate of Philosophy
from the University of Texas.

At six years old, Tommy learned not to put
his finger in another person's mouth,
even if he's asked. I wonder if that
incident long ago influenced
his decision to pursue his doctorate?
If it did, I don't believe he'd thank me.

Do I regret that it happened? No, I don't.
All of us have regrets. What one
assimilates from the experience is
far more important than the misgiving itself.
It's the nature of regret.

We each learned lessons
from that impetuous act.
Something we both wouldn't have
if I hadn't bitten his finger.

Harry Truman

An old codger, not the former president.
Caretaker of the Mt. Saint Helens Lodge
at the foot of Spirit Lake for 52 years.

Surviving the
torpedoing of the Tuscania
in 1918 off the coast of Ireland.
He'd seen the face of danger before.

Tremors threw him out of bed,
so he moved his mattress to the basement.
He scoffed at the public's concern for his safety.
No matter how hard everyone coaxed,
he was steadfast. At 84, he proclaimed
"If the mountain goes, I'm going with it!"
Along with his 16 cats.

On May 18, 1980, he did just that.
The most significant US volcanic eruption
in 65 years. Depositing ash in 11 states.
Turning the lush green and russet forest
into dank charcoal grey.

His friend, John Garrity, remarked,
*"If he'd left and saw what the mountain did to
his lake, it would have killed him anyway."*

Some people pass with a whimper,
others in pain with their pangs.
He did not go gentle into the night,
but truly went out with a bang.

Once They've Seen Paree

In 1917, the United States needed soldiers
to enter World War One.
The Selective Service Act registered
all males aged 21 to 30,
and 4.8 million men were drafted –
including blacks – truly second class citizens,
known then as Negroes.

They served in the cavalry, infantry
signal, medical, engineer and
artillery units. And as chaplains,
chemists, truck drivers, surveyors
and intelligence officers.
Europeans welcomed all American troops
with little or no distinction
between black or white.
It was a new world many Negroes
had never seen or experienced.
They reveled in newly found respect,
finding a true taste of freedom
on the French front lines.

And then, the Great War was over.
Armistice took effect and our soldiers –
all our soldiers – began coming home.
That's when trouble began.
Good old boys wanted everything
back to the way it was.
But black soldiers had seen
the way things ought to be.
Rude awakening for *"uppity"* Negro war heroes.
Race riots erupted in 26 cities
with 77 confirmed lynchings –
some hanged veterans still in uniform.

In 1948, President Harry Truman
desegregated the military.

How will our Negroes come back home
and know their place
once they've seen Paree?

The Letter

With Dad passing,
I took on the task of going through
my parent's pictures and papers
accumulated in their
sixty-four years of marriage.
A formidable responsibility.
Keeping some for prosperity.
Discarding others for eternity.
Onus of judge and jury.

As I sojourned forth
on my fifth and final box,
I came across a small letter
addressed to my parents,
dated June 8, 1970.
To my surprise, it was about me.
And my poetry.

Why they kept it from me,
I'll never know.
Yet, here it was, discovered,
forty-eight years later.

I faintly remember Miss Kristianson.
A substitute for the last couple months
of my junior year poetry course.
She made words come alive in class.
I recall loving her enthusiasm.
Her encouragement. Her smiles.
My words, in her eyes, were worthwhile.
A lofty compliment for a boy of sixteen.
Our paths never crossed again.

It took a few Google searches,
but I located her phone number
and called her out of the blue.
I told her about the letter I had found –
and how much it must have meant to my folks.
She was back at her parent's old home in Redmond
after taking care of her Alzheimer-ridden mother.
She had a handicapped child herself,
now institutionalized at Fircrest School.

She had become a special education teacher –
finally retiring from that career.

I told her I had made my career from writing –
one way or the other – in many jobs and passions
that filled my pursuits and livelihoods.

I explained how much her positivity meant to me
back then
and what a wonderful surprise
the long-forgotten letter was now.
I sent her two of my published poetry books
which I hope she'll read
and then remember fondly
that bright-eyed sixteen year-old boy.

June 8, 1970

Dear Mr. and Mrs. Bruneau:

I'm writing this to you on behalf
of your son, Ed. I have been sub-
stituting this past school year at
Redmond High School and have been
very impressed by the excellent
poetry your son writes. I also
write poetry and was impressed by
the excellent quality of his work.
It is superior to a great deal of
published poetry.

I felt his poetry should be published.
I recommend that he send a manuscript
of ten or twenty poems to either
Mr. Nelson Bentley, a well known
Northwest poet and also a professor
at the University of Washington) or
Dr. Zillman (I've forgotten his first
name), who is also a professor at
the University of Washington in the
English Department. He teaches
about the two poets, William Wordsworth
and Samuel Coleridge. Both of these
men are also involved in the publica-
tion of a poetry magazine called
Northwest Poetry Review. You could
address it to either of their names
and send it in care of Padelford Hall,
English Dep't., U. of Washington.

I also mentioned to Ed that he
start sending his poetry for publi-
cation to various magazines- also
his short stories. There is a

-2-

magazine published monthly called
Poetry Digest or a similar title
which can be found at Marketime
Drugstores. It tells their addresses,
what type of poetry they market, the
amount paid per line, and approximately
the length of poems they desire.

I'm very sure that Ed has the innate
ability and talent to be one of our
best future poets. His poetry (at
this early stage) has universal
application and any individual can
identify with it. This is poetry
that can be read by everyone and each
person can recognize his own feelings
within its contents.

I'm presently working on a project
which will be part of my thesis work.
It is concerned with poetic creativity
and because of this, I could see even
more clearly the tremendous talent
your son portrays in his work.

I hope you do not find this too bold
to have written this letter. I have
always loved the area of English and
the fascinating game of words and their
order in relationship to creating poetry
so that I felt compelled to write this
letter to you as Ed's parents in order
that you could encourage him to send his
material in manuscript form to various
persons and magazines that could make
his work known to the public.

Sincerely,

Miss Sunne Kristianson

Be Gone, Winter

Spring, where art thou?
Your sparkling personality
and smiling face
usually arrives by now.

March winds seldom
take holiday into April –
a clueless guest who makes its nest.
Outstays our genuine welcome.

Be gone, winter.
You've lingered far too long.
Flagrant freeloader. Jubilant joker.
Let spring sing its fragrant song.

What can we do to be rid of you?
Nudge you down the cobbled path?
Or find a way to abort your stay –
dash out your desperate last gasp.

We must contain our yearn for spring –
budding flowers, birds and bees.
There's nothing we can really do
until you finally decide to leave.

Spring Forward

Yesterday, my neighbor pointed out
the first buttercups in his yard.
He said he was already
weeks behind in tree pruning
and, budding or not,
they were going to get haircuts.

It's time, isn't it?
Spring cleaning. Spring planting.
Marigold and geranium seeds
already sprouting indoors
under LED grow lights.
Donna caught spring fever
more than a month ago
and uncovered the plants,
raking off leaves and pine needles
which protected the perennials.
Then, the weather turned cold
and we got snow again,
up through the first days of March.

That's what spring does.
We want it to come so desperately,
sometimes we're a bit too eager.
It's time for new leaves,
baby birds, beetles, bunnies, bees.
Our world goes from grey to green.
Of course it's something to look forward to.
We even moved our clocks ahead an hour today
to enjoy another precious hour of daylight.

Spring is a wonderful reminder
not to take the kitten out of the cat
or the wild out of the child.

Summer comes rapidly enough.
It all grows up too soon.

Staying in Bed

Today I decided
to not get out of bed.
Weighed all the downsides.
Chose the advantages instead.
I can just lie here.
Pretend I'm dead.
Stay under the comfy covers.
Won't face the day with dread.

Don't have to worry about
fresh underwear or socks.
Avoid choosing a shirt or pants.
Crazy, like a fox.
No breakfast to make.
Nor lunch or dinner, for that matter.
No dishes to clean or pans to wash.
I'll end up thinner, not fatter.

I'll plant myself right here.
Pull the sheet over my head.
Evade hearsay for just one day.
Leave the newspaper unread.
No phone or computer.
No contact with the outside world.
Just want to sidestep it all.
Elude the bustle and the whirl.

Erase the day from the calendar.
Put all worries in deletion.
For once, I will simply stay in bed.
Feign off rhyme and reason.
Curtail all feeling and emotion.
Enjoy just being numb.
Today, I'll sleep the day away.
Face tomorrow when it comes.

Clouds with Ashen Lining

Dreary day taps rain upon my window.
Drummers' cadence march in revolution.
Puddles simmering erratic effervescence.
Grey coats colors dull in charcoal pastels.

Mood plummets into sinking fog,
clutching whatever hope may survive
before abandoning ship into darkness.

I draw curtains closed and switch on lamps,
where color again emerges, artificial and dim.
Forget about rain, embrace the cocoon.
Plant warm leather under my seat and
settle in, studying schematics for flying cars
from a 1954 Mechanix Illustrated.

Radio drowns out dampened drummers –
soothing slumber of *Cristofori's Dream.*

My-gration

Time to find another path
along this road more traveled.
Leave the lemmings far behind,
give new direction a gamble.
Separate from the flock,
start the flight anew.
Don't give it a second thought.
Leave them in the rearview.

Search for fledging promise.
This time it's for you.
No matter what someone says,
It's really yours to pursue.
Open the door to possibility.
Close the door on doubt.
No matter what you encounter
you'll always work it out.

Some just aimlessly wander.
Some let the road take them.
Some explore what's yonder –
make memories, new friends.
Pioneer the great unknown.
Go beyond uncertainty.
Without risk, you have no chance
to spend your future currency.

New Year

Advancing into the new year
makes me reflect on the year past –
Melancholy loss
of family, of friends, of furry companions.
Goals achieved. Expectations denied.
All boxed up for storage,
tied with a fancy bow.

Advancing into the new year
delivers a clean slate –
new adventures into the unknown.
Plethora of possibilities.
New resolves. New positivity.
Optimism. Promise. Hope.
A new energy
as winter begins to shed her cloak.

It's all made up, really –
this marker within the passage of time.
It could be any point in our 365 day cycle
which would rewind and repeat
the certain upcoming seasons
and the uncertainty of tomorrows.

The Roman Calendar named
January from Janus –
the god of beginnings, gates, transitions,
duality, doorways, passages and endings.
He has two faces,
looking to both the future and the past.

Advancing into the new year,
the past is behind me but not forgotten.
The future will be learned a day at a time
until it too becomes a box,
tied with a fancy bow.

Terra Cotta Heart

Thought it was
bloody red like mine.
Turns out I was mistaken.
Yours was hardened
reddish brown
and I, the one, forsaken.

Sought the truth
from seers and sooths.
Never was I selfish.
Turned it around,
made a fool of me.
My labor, all but rubbish.

Stone cold
your terra cotta heart,
under pink vinyl skin.
Wounded by callous cruelty –
your merciless insensitivity.
I bleed outward and within.

It's Quiet Now

She could fill the vacuum of silence
with ease, especially with those stories
we had all heard so many times before.
She told it like it was the first time,
every time. It didn't matter if you listened.
Silence haunted her. Tortured her.
Compelling her to spew verbal vomit
over anyone in earshot. When she talked
she could no longer hear the quiet.
The lull. The hush. The still. The sullenness.
Self-medicating her disease.
She couldn't help herself. Yet,
all close to her suffered as well,
bearing the brunt of her anxiety
by her constant drone of discourse,
drowning out one's own thoughts.
Suffocating the souls of her offspring.
The damage metastasized.

The oldest, Linda, left first, from bone cancer –
a two pack a day Benson & Hedges smoker.
Then Mary Lou, a primary school teacher,
succumbs to ovarian cancer. Then Susie,
her youngest, from that asbestos cancer,
mesothelioma. Then Cheryl, second oldest,
a casualty of severe multiple sclerosis.
Finally Dixie, a registered nurse, perishes
from pancreatic cancer at 68.

She outlived all but one of her six daughters.
On Friday, passing away herself at age 97.
Audrey joins her children once again
in a place where silence is revered
and her own torment vanquished.

Purgatory

A charcoal sketch
with resemblance.
Instinct instead
of routine.
A guest in his
own residence.
Stuck somewhere
in-between.
Hard to remember yesterday.
Calendar confusion.
A sigh overrides
his normal smile.
An inconvenient intrusion.
Not all things
improve with age
like a bottle of fine wine.
Sometimes they decompose.
Some before their time.
Familiar fades more everyday -
fewer stories he can tell.
It's a blessing he doesn't remember.
Resigns to existence
not in heaven.
Not in hell.

Mirror Mirror

Down is the new up.
Left is the new right.
Right is the new wrong.
Digital is the new analog.
Rap is the new Shakespeare.
Purchase is the new repair.
Fake is the new news.
Subjectivity is the new truth.
Media is the new defiance.
Phones are the new intimacy.
Insincerity is the new genuine.
Ambiguity is the new certainty.
Politics are the new larceny.
Weed is the new intoxicant.
Binge-watching is the new drug.
Internet is the new dating.
Gender is the new carnal knowledge.
Diversion is the new conformity.
Polarization is the new community.
Intolerance is the new understanding.
Illegals are the new sanctuary.
Apathy is the new impotence.
Bitcoin is the new money.
Terrorism is the new religion.

The world is inverted, backwards, alas –
It's tough to peer through
a cracked looking glass.

The Great Pumpkin

He is the mystery behind
this haunting holiday.
The day when trepidation
collides with invitation –
bribed with candy
and other tricks and treats.

Some families find it
imprudent to participate
in pagan proceedings –
rooted from the
Gaelic harvest festival,
launching the year's darker half.

Stores sell sugar galore.
Bite-size morsels for
the Halloween bowl –
Anonymously disappearing
long before the
ghosts and goblins arrive.

The Great Pumpkin fails to come.
A humiliated, but undefeated Linus
vows to wait for him again
the following Halloween.
We are all still waiting for our
presidential pumpkin to rise up
in the political patch as well.

Trump

There once was a man named Trump
who said he wanted a sump pump.
He needed to drain
the swamp that remained
but now it's just a big dump.

Warm White Light

A few days after she died
I felt her presence around me
like a warm white light
wanting to hang around,
making sure I would be alright.
It was a comfortable feeling,
her spirit with me,
making funeral planning
and all the other
difficult decisions of death
less depressing than
it all could have been.

The warm white light
illuminating my Maui retreat
and lifting my morning meditations,
praying for celestial guidance.
New roads from here,
I thought to myself.
Directing me to the right paths
while the next chapter is
already in progress.

The warm white light
followed me back to the homeland,
making the adjustment to the
nightmare of normalcy
less painful than
it all could have been.
She knew Donna from
our award ceremonies
and the warm white light
surged when we were together.

In the weeks afterward
as we got to know each other better,
the warm white light began to fade,
slowly retreating over time,
fearful of saying goodbye
but realizing
I would indeed be alright.

I'm sitting in the railway station.
Got a ticket to my destination.
On a tour of one-night stands, my suitcase and guitar in hand.
And every stop is neatly planned
for a poet and a one-man band.
– Paul Simon, Homeward Bound

Homeward Bound

I'm the poet, not the one man band.
At every stop, I await the
reception that isn't there.
No official greeting.
No honorary key to the hamlet.
No welcome wagon.

I move about through
a crowd of pedestrians
politely avoiding me
as if I'm a nuisance –
a regrettable, faceless extra
set among the cast
of their own movie –
where I have no lines.

On the barstool next to me,
two thumbs enamored deeply
in a text conversation.
The jukebox fiddles
a sad country tune
and I realize I located
the one man band.

Home is still far away,
but headed homeward
makes me dream of
my movie, my direction,
my cast of characters.

This poet longs for
the familiar.
Comfortable slippers
embraced by the
warmth hearth of home.

Hideaway

When the world
collapses and crumbles,
what satisfies
the stress?

When words
reduce to mumble.
Discord you
can't express.

When there's no
end in the tunnel,
no light to
see success...

It's time to find
a hideaway,
a sanctuary
from duress.

My hideaway is quiet.
Peaceful. Tranquil.
Undisturbed.
A place to charge
my batteries,
my own thoughts
easily heard.

I know that I
can't stay here.
Must heal and
face the day.
But I steal a
small memento
that soothes me
from dismay.

Two to Tango

My mother always used to say,
"It takes two to tango."
Such a strange thing to say,
especially to a child.
But the more I've gotten older,
the more the idiom rings true.
The gate does swing both ways.
And it's a two-way street, too.

Love is like a simple dance
where each heart does its part.
The dancing stops when
we're out of step.
From then,
it may never start.

It does take two to tango.
Easy to get off on the wrong foot.
We were like two peas in a pod.
Now the relationship is kaput.

Two wrongs don't make a right.
Two heads are better than one.
Two can play at this game.
The lesser of two evils is none.

I put in my two cents.
I stand on my own two feet.
It may take two to tango,
but there's no victory in defeat.

When two people can't hear the music,
it's time to find someone else to dance.
In two shakes of a lamb's tail,
it's worth taking the chance.

Animus

I think I would rather be
a boulder than a pebble.
Strive for truth in rich pursuit
than surrender and sadly settle.
Be the scent of flower sweet
rather than the petal.
Make goodwill a prevailing wind
in lieu of being special.
Help the hungry find some food,
but not supply their mettle.
Straighten out the knotted lines.
Puzzle pieces to assemble.
Join the side of angelic ideal
than the conceal of the devil.

A person's purpose.
A chance for difference –
more than just a speckle.
A spirit far beyond one's grasp,
with you and me, the vessel.

Hot Water

It was my feeble attempt at humor
that skewed it in the first place.
You get one chance
to make a first impression –
and it was going sideways immediately.
I just smiled. Sometimes that will help
get out of a jam. Not this time.
No, this time I totally stepped in it.
May Day. May Day. Send out the S.O.S.
Call the Calvary. Beam me up Scotty.
But it was no use. No rewind. No escape.
I had to face the music and
eat that horrible humble pie.
Sit there and take the punishment.
Let the venom cascade over me
like a cold shower. It will be over soon.
Then I can slither away like a snake and
retreat under a rock, my sanctuary.
Where I can begin to forget it ever happened.
Let echoes of the encounter fade away and
disappear into faint memory – where
I finally forgive myself, remembering
all of us are, after all, only human.

Whisper in the Wind

I couldn't make out the whisper –
the whisper in the wind.
Maybe it was a warning.
Maybe just a hint.
Its voice – set too softly
to hear what it had to say.
Was it a crucial message?
A commandment to obey?
It wasn't my imagination –
something there I heard.
A whisper, faint and distant –
couldn't make out the words.
I wanted to hear the whisper again,
listen closer to its content.
I waited for the message to return,
reinterpret the intent.

Alas, there was no replay.
It never reappeared.
My one chance to understand –
lost forever, I fear.

If you are ever fortunate enough
to receive a whisper in the wind,
tune it in and listen hard
or get caught up in the chagrin.

Dichotomy Debris

A portion of truth
makes the lie digestible.

The truth, the whole truth
and nothing but the truth.
Dreams and greed make
the improbable suggestible.

If it's too good to be true,
it often is.
If you repeat it often enough
the perception is factual.

Insanity is doing the same
thing over and over and
expecting a different result.
Tell them what they want to hear,
they'll believe the words are actual.

A naked truth is better
than a well dressed lie.
The more pleasant the words,
the more persuasive.

More flies are caught
with honey than vinegar.
No truth is absolute.
Everything is relative.

Lies stand on one leg.
The truth on two.
People believe the big lie
rather than the small one.

The longer the explanation
the bigger the lie.
The strong take some convincing.
The weak simply just succumb.

Truth fears no questions.

Good Grief

I noticed you had a suitcase.
Are you staying for a while?
You somehow know when I need you.
When my heart is breaking.
When someone I love has left me.
When I must go on without.

Come in, dear grief.
Hold my hand in my sadness.
Comfort me in my tears.
Slow my steps and make me pause –
to reflect upon my loss
and the joy I did not intend
to take for granted.

Stay with me, my grief,
until I'm ready to say goodbye.
Until I'm ready to let go.
Until I can put all the memories
in a special, safe place
where I can visit again
without weeping.

I listen to your counsel, grief.
You tell me nothing really ends.
That life must go on.
That everything has a purpose.
I argue with you out of sorrow,
saying things I know are not true.
But your gentle persuasion prevails.

I know it's time for you to leave, grief.
I don't want to see you go.
Can you stay just one more day?
Let's toast your farewell with a nice merlot.
Part as friends and say goodbye.
Until I you knock again.

Hamlet Heartbreak

There they are, outside our window.
Plundering the terrain
with mechanical dinosaurs
and other earth-moving monsters.
Laying the groundwork for a
twenty-new-home infrastructure
from 7am until 6pm daily.

When my nincompoop of a neighbor
sold their four-and-a-half acre farm
to the marauding developer,
it was certainly an act of treason.
Upsetting the natural order
of our stomping ground –
creating havoc with
our normal peace and quiet.

Gone is the privacy
we once took for granted.
Now, a panoramic view
of tire tracks and mud
replace the pastoral pasture.
Sounds of war –
booms, bangs and beeps
awaken us instead of an alarm.

Our hamlet's serenity
and scenery
robbed and ransacked
in the name of progress.
Why does it feel like
rape and plunder instead?

Futile Fantasia

He was only ten years old
when he began to draw.
Crude comic strips, pencil and ink.
Complete stories, start to end.
A fantasy world where he could be
the super hero or the villain.
Leave his lonely world behind.
Escape into his imagination.

There'd be the dream
he was the favorite child
and the new red bike was his
instead of baby brother's.
Maybe his parents would
put down their Pall Malls –
praise the clever cartoons.
Encourage him to do another.

No matter how many he drew
he could not change his place.
Pages and pages. Volumes of work.
Didn't shift his fate.
They ignored the budding talent.
Neglected his moment to shine.
Ended up a janitor.
Sweeping the dust, dirt and grime.

One can only wonder who he would be –
a different place, another family.
Cultivated and supported,
watching his blossoms bloom.
The kid drawing comic strips –
grounded by earth's gravity
instead of shooting for the moon.

Haunted

There's a ghost in our house.
Making floors creek
at three o'clock in the morning.
A friendly spirit, this rascal.
Who seems satisfied
to gently haunt us
without any harm.
Just a door slam.
Or sudden chill.
Subtle nuances
that let us know
it's still around.
When something ends up missing,
it wasn't misplaced.
Just the ghost
manipulating some madness
until it's finally found.
Our cat Zippy
could sense the spook
and would meow outside
the guest bedroom door
for hours.
But our phantom pundit left us.
Joining the apparition
in its ethereal mission
to continue to be
a part of our lives –
even if only in the shadows.

Journey to Humus

On the ground – leaves galore.
Signal of the season.
Each leaf departing
the security of a branch
at the moment
it can wait no longer –
joining the calamity
of fellow brethren
on earth's floor.
Dancing to the
slightest breeze
in green vibrancy
fades to evanescence.
Now gold. Now old.
Destiny now
decomposition and decay.
A journey to humus.
Chowder for the fungi.

Simba

There was a time
in your earliest days
when you weren't
the picture of health.
We both worried about you,
but I
catered the evening hours
as she slept,
exhausted from day's toil.
I made you a promise
as I held you,
a tiny soul in my arms.
I would always be there
when you needed me.
I would get you through
physical or mental trauma.
And be your strength
until you became a man.
Capable of your own decisions.
Handling your own affairs.
Making your own victories and mistakes.
You grew from a sapling
into a strong, majestic oak.
I am proud
of living out the promise I made
and seeing you thrive.

Syzygy

S-Y-Z-Y-G-Y.
It was my father's favorite word.
When I was young we'd play hangman
and he would stump us with
this mysterious word with the three "y's"
He's use it for Scrabble or any other excuse.
I think he loved the unusual magic of it.

A syzygy is a straight-line configuration
of three celestial bodies
in a gravitational system.

An eclipse is a syzygy.

It was the second day of his hospital stay
and he had read about the phenomenon
in the newspaper – and heard numerous
reports on the television news.
Don't look directly into the sun!
Don't look directly into the sun!
It echoed in his 87-year-old mind.
Although totality was 230 miles away,
93 percent of the sun would be covered
by the moon outside his room's window.
In the state he was in, his mind confused
looking at the sun with even being outdoors.
He warned me on the phone not to go outside.
My sister made sure
his room's blinds were drawn
and curtains closed so he wouldn't fear
losing his eyesight to this
disturbing eclipse event.
Fortunately, he slept through it.
Eight days later, he was gone.

His life had eclipsed from his
tired, worn-out earthly body,
releasing his spirit into the celestial –
where he again would align himself
among the planets, moon and stars
and transcend into a million syzygys,
guiding each in place within the universe.

Peacock

The pompous peacock
bathes in his reflection –
procures a glorious plume
in primp and proper perfection.

Aviary arrogance,
this technicolor fowl.
Insufferable when others inquire
not just why, but how?

Shielded from reality,
vanity needs a buffer.
Smugness is his cup of tea
while you and I simply suffer.

Trumped up conceit, this brazen bird,
fans its feathers for fascination.
Followers want a megalomaniac
chief executive of our nation.

Holds himself in high regard,
head too big for hat.
I'll be glad when his term's done
and no longer put up with that.

Powerless

A candle burns by the window,
flickers a beacon beckoning.
Home is alive and waiting in the dark
for night's welcome – never ever.

A child's colored chalk masterpiece
washes away in the rain,
leaves a fading pastel remembrance
of what was once inspiration.

Powerless drawing attention to the flame.
Powerless preserving precious sidewalk art.
Ubiquitous disappointment
of self-created expectations.

Reality too raw to cope –
a struggling human frailty.
Withdrawing into the
cocoon of our own denial.

Stroke of Luck

Things were going on quite normally
before my mind turned less robust.
I couldn't speak the words I wanted –
you might say I was quite nonplused!
I tried to write a simple poem
and couldn't put two words together.
Something was wrong, couldn't respond,
was messed up by any measure.
First an ultrasound, then an MRI
and a CAT Scan with contrast.
Doctor said they found the cause
and the problem had likely past.
No joke, it was actually a stroke.
A blood clot in my brain.
Handicapped by what I lacked.
Would I ever be the same?
75 milligrams of Plavix daily
would help prevent another.
Words began coming back to me
which was wonderful to discover.
I thank my angels and fairies
for my good fortune to recover.
Nothing's worse than such a curse
turning mental mastery into butter.

Slender Circumstance

A man pauses to read his watch,
missing a stray bullet by an inch.
Right time, wrong place.
It wasn't his time.
But a ripple flows beyond
this miraculous near miss.
The bullet penetrates
a coffee shop window,
puncturing a hole
in the espresso machine,
severely scalding two baristas.
Wrong time, right place.
It was their time.
On the way to the hospital,
a semi-truck fails to yield the siren.
The ambulance crushed
like a ball of tin foil,
while packages of frozen french fries
destined for Japan
cover the roadway
causing a traffic jam for hours.
Wrong time, wrong place.

If the man hadn't stopped for a moment
there would have been no scalding.
Or accident. Or traffic jam.
Or shortage in the
french fry export pipeline.
Just a stray bullet
lodged too near his kidney
for a successful operation.
We often think
little of what we do really matters –
when even the slightest,
most ordinary act
shifts ripples in a new direction
in ways we can never imagine.

Most decisions and actions
we make daily are
beyond our conscious control.
Some aren't.

Spring Fever

Remove snow tires.
Murder dandelions.
Blow driveway.
Decommission snowblower.
Schedule sprinklers.
Set wasp traps.
Call gutter guy,
window guy,
tree guy,
shrub pulling guy,
exterminator.
Open greenhouse vent.
Nurse tomatoes, basil,
marigolds and
lemon cucumbers
until time to plant.
Rototill garden.
Buy 36 bags of bark.
Get propane for
fireplace and barbecue.
Place 48 solar lights.
Kill gravel weeds.
Kill gravel weeds.
Kill gravel weeds.
Repeat.
Fertilize lawn.
Use sunscreen.
Enjoy gin & tonic on patio.

Welcome the
sacraments of spring.

Mordant Memories

Dyed in my wool.
Memories I won't forget.
As time passes on,
I will remember.

When I'm old,
I will reminisce –
even if I can't recall what I ate
for breakfast that morning.

Like a colorful blanket design,
fading, losing brilliance over time,
it remains within the fabric
that has woven my life.

The hurdle of aging
faces us all, eventually.
Going forth flimsy without
the effervescence of youth.

My milestones and
disappointments
are my story. My DNA.
My unique imprint.

Let age rob me of
my vulnerability.
Provide the essence
of my obsolescence.

Just let the memories remain,
embedded within –
the tapestry of my definition intact,
covering my corpse when I depart.

Ode to the Commode

Some people call it latrine.
Water closet.
Or toilet.
But it's better than
an outhouse –
keeping all it's kept.
No, the commode
wooshes it all away
in one easy flush.
Where it goes,
no one knows,
If you did –
it's likely to disgust.
A place to
do your business.
The throne from
which you rule.
But I'm glad it's there
at 3am
in its private vestibule.
A modern miracle.
A porcelain imperative.
If you have problems
using it, you probably
need a laxative.
All in all this
dandy device rises
above its bad rap.
What other appliance
will serve you best
when you give it
a lot of
crap?

Ceremony of Tears

The Natives called it "the great flood." But it was more than that. Much more. A renowned fishing spot for over 7,000 years was gone – flooded by the backwaters of the new Coulee Dam.

Natives say the salmon were once so plentiful one could walk across the river on their backs. In season, fisherman captured up to 3,000 fish in a single day. It was a gathering place of tribes. Where people met, got married, had babies and settled disputes.

Tribes also mourned the destruction of thousands of acres of food-producing bottomlands – a major source for the traditional diet of roots and berries.

Now the magnificent Kettle Falls was no more, buried 90 feet below the surface. Salmon no longer had a way to migrate past the dam. It was over. As were the ancient graves of the Natives' forefathers. Gone. Buried again below the ice blue waters of Lake Roosevelt.

That's where my story begins. If I hadn't experienced it with my own eyes, I wouldn't have believed it myself. But it's true.

I was a security guard during the dam's third powerplant expansion in 1970. By then, the huge new facility had been built, but the generators had not been installed yet. It was a big, open space, sparse of the technology soon to come. Inside, it was quiet. Deathly so. And unfortunately, my transistor radio couldn't get a signal while inside the thick concrete walls. In fact, it was a problem for everyone there. Workers inside would sing. Or hum. Anything to break the maddening silence.

Unfortunately, I had a shift they called the "graveyard." I began work at 10:00 pm and went home at 6:00 in the morning. The shift had the fewest workers and of course, the greatest silence. It was also the time when people were rumored to see and hear things that shouldn't have been there. Now I can't confirm or deny what other people saw. But I can tell you what happened to me.

The middle of June was unusually hot, even for Eastern Washington standards. That made the evenings pleasantly warm as well. But it was always cool inside the plant.

I just finished my first rounds about midnight when I began to barely hear something quite out of the ordinary. Drums. First, I had thought it might have been some kind of hammering or workers installing gear, but it was too precise. Too rhythmic. And then the chanting began. I instantly knew it wasn't just a worker singing a song.

Even though my next rounds weren't supposed to begin until 3:00 am, I decided to do them early and see if I could detect where these strange sounds were coming from. There were eight floors in the plant and I was going to check all of them out, one at a time.

The sounds seem to get a little louder as I descended down each floor. When I finally got to the bottom area, I walked into the chamber and discovered an amazing sight. Dozens of Native Americans, maybe about 40 in all, in a large circle where a huge turbine generator would soon be installed. Some were dancing in ceremony, others were chanting or beating drums. I, of course, wondered how in the heck they had gotten in here – specifically, how they all got past me. And there was a large bonfire in the middle. But no smoke. Now, that's really odd, I thought.

One of the natives detected my presence. I didn't know whether to flee or pull out my pistol. I was frozen in my tracks. But he motioned with his arm in a manner that seemed to say, "join us." Reluctantly, I slowly stepped toward the circle and sat next to a very elderly man in headdress who had been beating a drum. He handed me his instrument and motioned that I should play with the others. At this point, I figured I had better do as I was told.

The chanting was in a language I didn't understand. But as I played the drum and watched the dance for a while, the foreign words suddenly began to make sense to me. First it was a song about the ancients who had reaped the abundance of the land and returned to the earth as the soil. Then the sentiment suddenly turned sad and I could clearly understand in my mind the new chant that cried, "No more. No more. No more."

The old man next to me was crying. The chanting stopped and he stood up to speak. He had the attention of everyone there, including me. I know he was talking in his native tongue, but by some kind of bewitchment, I understood what he was saying.

He said he had been the "Chief of the Waters" and had opened every season by spearing the first fish. He was the one who divided the catch among the families at the end of each day. And he began sobbing, which interrupted his speech for several minutes. No one else in the circle made a sound. "This is the place that created the flood. This is the place that stopped the salmon. This is the place that buried our sacred ancients underwater and moved our tribes to higher ground," he explained. "This is our Ceremony of Tears. It honors the life we had for thousands of years and lets us weep over its demise."

I stayed with them until it was almost time for me to go home. He had motioned that we bow our heads in a type of prayer. I closed my eyes. And when I opened them, they were gone. The fire was gone. It was just me, sitting in the huge circle where the new generator was to be installed. And it was silent once again.

I didn't go home that morning. I called my wife and told her I had to work another shift, but of course that wasn't true. I drove to Electric City Tavern and started drowning my own thoughts in suds – good ol' Olympia beer. I wasn't sure of my own sanity. Did I really experience these Native American spirits or did I just fall asleep during my watch and dream it? And even if it was true, how could I tell anyone? They'd put me in a padded room for sure, I thought.

I crawled out of the tavern just as the lunch crowd was coming in and immediately went home to bed and passed out. My wife woke me up for dinner about 8:30pm and I put on my uniform again and headed to work. I was reluctant to go back on this night to what had been a very routine job. But I did anyway.

Sure enough, about midnight again, I heard the same sounds as the night before.

I took the elevator eight floors down and went into the generator room. I still could hear the drums and chants. But to my surprise, there was just one fella there, warming himself by a burn barrel. Again, there were flames, but no smoke. I came up to him to see him better. He also looked Native American, but this time in ordinary, sorta shabby clothes.

"Who goes there?" I said. "How do you people keep getting passed security?"

"What people?" he asked. "It's just me."

"Nevermind that," I stated. "Who are you?"

"Private First Class Thomas William Desautel, sir, 11th Regiment, U.S. Marines," he replied.

"Do you know where you are?" I asked.

"The Dam. Grand Coulee. It got me on March the 7th, 1940." Desautel frowned. "Not a lot of jobs, then. You took what you could get. Even dangerous ones. You can call me Tom."

So Tom began to tell me the story of his life. How he grew up on the reservation. How he served his country as a truck driver in World War One. How times were hard after the war and employment was scarce. "Especially for an Indian," he explained.

Then he got a job working on the dam beginning in 1933. "Hard work and fair pay for seven years," he recalled. "But I was helping with filling in the cracks with concrete grout on the upper portion of the dam and my feet fell out in front of me. It was a spectacular fall."

I told Tom what I had experienced the night before. Even about the Ceremony of Tears. Ironically, his view of the situation was different. "Germany was marching into Paris and France was falling to Hitler," Desautel remembered. "We needed more power so we could build more airplanes, ships and tanks. War was coming. Many of us veterans knew that. FDR knew that. Grand Coulee Dam was part of a plan bigger than all of us. It was a plan to protect the United States. And put fear into Hitler's cold heart."

"So, what about your brethren?" I asked. "The salmon gone. Sacred sites drowned – disappeared underwater. Entire villages relocated. What of that?"

Tom became quiet. We sat together by the burn barrel and said nothing. Then he spoke. "I'd like to think my life made a difference. That what I did was worthwhile. Sometimes that means change. What if there were salmon and no dams but we all had to talk German instead? Would Swastikas and Nazis been a better world?"

The drums and the chanting continued, still out of nowhere. The sound surrounded us. I put my arm over Tom's shoulder. "Thank you," I said. "Thank you for your service to our country. And yes, I do think you made a difference."

Tom looked up to me – his sad eyes turned into a wistful stare. "I wish it hadn't had to be that way," he shrugged. "Salmon kept my people alive in the winter months. Sometimes there are no easy answers."

We talked quietly together until the wee hours of morning. He looked at me and told me he had to go. The drumming and chanting stopped. And suddenly, he and the burn barrel were gone, leaving me sitting alone once again in the generator room.

Just before I punched out, I walked into my supervisor's office. I told him I wanted a week off. He just made a notation in his tablet and said, "Fine, see you in a week." He didn't ask why. I found out later this had happened many times before. I wasn't the only one. But no one ever filed a report. Once in a while, after suds at Electric City Tavern, a patron might mention something about seeing some Indians at work, but it was always hushed up by his fellow co-workers. It was best not said. No one would believe any of us, anyway.

When I returned after my week 'vacation', things were pretty much back to normal. The turbine generator was to be installed that week and from that moment on, there was no longer any regular silence in the giant concrete bunker we all worked in. And I stayed employed in the security office until I retired a decade later. I never did see any more Native Americans who weren't supposed to be there. Or hear again those eerie drums and chants that haunted me for those two shifts long ago.

But there's a *Twilight Zone* ending to my tale. In retirement, I enjoyed going to our local library – catching up on reading I missed out on during my working years. One day I did more research about Kettle Falls and discovered that on June 14, 1940, there was a gathering of tribes at the site – some say up to 8,000 to 10,000 people. It was called the 'Ceremony of Tears' to commemorate the soon-to-be-lost ancient fishing site.

And sure enough, among the list of workers who died during the construction of the Grand Coulee Dam Project was a fellow by the name Thomas William Desautel.

Invalid Votes Found

Election In Doubt

by Brian Mottaz and
Julie Kittleson

At least 19 votes cast in the AS general election April 25 are invalid due to a constitutional requirement dealing with full-fee paying students. Invalidation of those votes may require the entire election or parts of it to be held over again especially that part dealing with the constitutional amendments.

The Easterner has determined that at least 19 persons voting in the general election were not eligible to vote based on a constitutional provision dealing with the amount of tuition paid by a student.

Only "members" of the AS are eligible to vote in any election and the constitution defines members of the AS as being "all students who are full-fee paying students of Eastern Washington State College."

However, at least 19 persons voting in the last general election are carrying fewer than 10 credits—the cutoff point between full and part time student. Also, the 19 were either billed for only partial tuition or authorized for a refund if they had withdrawn from classes prior to the 30th calendar day of spring quarter which was April 26.

Not being full-fee paying students, their votes cannot be counted as valid according to the AS constitution, an AS spokesman said. The seven constitutional amendments on the general election ballot would be affected most by the 19 invalid votes.

A 20 percent voter turnout as well as a majority of yes votes are needed for passage of any constitutional amendments. In other words, 1,087 full-fee paying students must have voted in the general election for the amendments to be validated.

However, if the 19 invalid votes are counted, it brings the final election down to 1,085, or two votes under the 20 percent needed to validate the election.

However, it is possible the AS legislature may not take action on this situation, at least not right away, in light of developments at a meeting of the legislature late yesterday afternoon.

The AS had determined there were some invalid votes cast in the primary which could alter the outcome of that election. This information was presented to the legislature yesterday and three motions were made for possible action. All failed.

Because of the close races in the campaign for president, secretary and executive coordinator of activities as well as for position II on the legislature, it was moved to rescind a prior validation of that phase of the primary by the legislature. In other words, rule that portion of the election invalid and run it again.

However, that motion eventually failed by a vote of 9 to 8. Two

more motions were made, one to rescind the entire general election—it failed 12 to 3- and to rescind the entire primary—it failed 13 to 6.

So, after a nearly two hour meeting, the legislature decided to take no action regarding invalid votes cast in the primary election and general. It might be noted that the legislature was unaware of the 19 invalid votes discovered by The Easterner at the time of yesterday's meeting.

Roger Reed, assistant attorney general for Eastern Washington, was also on hand for yesterday's meeting of the legislature. He is also the legal counsel for the college. He had recommended that if the legislature was to take any action on the situation, it should be to only rescind those portions of the primary mentioned earlier.

Reed also said there is no question that "full-fee paying students" as mentioned in the constitution are those not paying full tuition—the same status of the 19 voters found by The Easterner.

He also said that if any appeals are to be made of the legislature's action not to change the outcome of the elections, they would have to be made to the Board of Trustees. However, he said he doubted the board would reverse the legislature's decisions on the matter because body is recognized, in the constitution as the final authority in all matters dealing with elections.

Thus if any action is to come of the information found by The Easterner concerning the 19 invalid votes in the general election, it will have to come from the legislature.

The 19 voters ineligible to cast a ballot according to the constitution were found by crosscheck ing the voter registration forms signed at the polls with the student load list obtained from the registrar's office.

Several Easterner staff members were involved in the checking of some 1,000 names along with three volunteers—Wayne Boulac, Mark Cerlin and Jay Johnson. About 100 names were not checked due to the time factor.

The fee-paying status of the 19 was confirmed by the student accounting office in Showalter. However, the names are being withheld from print tp avoid causing any problems to those who voted unaware of the constitutional requirement. The names are available to any official entity checking the validity of the election.

Some check of the voter registration forms was made by the AS, but only for double votes and it failed to turn up anything.

the easterner

Vol. 23 No. 1 No. 25 May 10, 1973

Committee Tabs Lakers For Mascot

Eastern Washington State Lakers - How do you like it? You do? You don't? Well, it really doesn't matter what you think, because if the Board of Trustees passes the recommendation at their May 18 meeting the no-names will be named.

The decision was made by a committee composed of Walt Schaar, President of the Alumni Association, Daryl Hagie, Vice President of Student Services, Kenneth Dolan, Assistant to the President, Bob Anderson, Director of Athletics, Jeff Riddle, A.S. President, and Bennie Dupris, Indian Education Programs.

Dolan said the name was chosen because of the large number of lakes in this area and its recreational appeal. He also said the alternate names which had been voted for were considered, but "Lakers" seemed the most appropriate.

Parking Cries Die In Vote

It was evident at the City Council Meeting Tuesday that the effects of "The city of Cheney is going to screw you" campaign had worn off. Only a few students were at the post-election meeting and the councilman who said "I'm in a good fighting mood tonight" should have brought his punching bag.

But even though it looked like the problem of parking had disappeared it hadn't, and Councilman Tom Scott presented the recommendations formulated by the new parking committee composed of students, faculty, administration, councilmen, and businessmen.

Enforcing the present parking ordinances relating to alleys, crosswalks, etc., was the first recommendation. Then Scott told what the committee had decided so far as to restrictive parking measures and Councilman who has been an outspoken member of the council on this issue, commented that they were "pretty restrictive."

The discussion focused primarily on Fourth Street, because the new fire station is now occupied and the council described the situation as an emergency. Since Fourth Street is about 30 feet wide and a firetruck is over eight feet wide, there isn't enough room for a fire truck and another vehicle to pass each other. And

having to wait for a car to back up during a fire isn't exactly convenient.

So after much discussion the council amended the committees original recommendation and applied Code 1 (no parking on either side of street) to Fourth Street from A to H Street, and from H to Union Street on the northwesterly side. The recommendations of C, D, and Fifth Street were also considered and because the council was making so many changes they decided to let the committee prepare another recommendation with their changes in mind.

The committee was also informed that if they lingered this would be replaced by the first parking committee.

Scott said the committee was in agreement that the college didn't provide adequate parking facilities and that they should supply ample parking for any new buildings constructed. Then the council voted to send letters to the Board of Trustees reiterating this sentiment.

Frank Marksman and Rick Schierman are the student representatives on the parking committee and Schierman said that "we're 100 percent in favor of eliminating parking where safety is a question, but where asselics is a primary concern, as to removing student parking to beautify the city of Cheney, we're totally against it and will fight it to the hilt."

What's inside today

READ ABOUT ALL THE LATEST DASTARDLY DEEDS and felonious capers in this weeks Crime Check on page 2.

FIND OUT WHAT SOME EASTERN STUDENTS think about the Watergate scandal in the opinion poll on page 2.

NEXT YEAR "THE EASTERNER" will have a new editor. The identity of the person who will hold this prestigious and honor-

ed position can be found out in the story on page 2.

JACK MARGOLIS, THE AUTHOR OF "CHILD'S GARDEN OF GRASS" spoke to Eastern students last week. A story on what he had to say can be found on page 3.

REAL LIFE ELECTION SCANDALS and political intrigue can be found in the satire in the Issues and Opinions section of the paper.

Issues and Opinions - pages 4 and 5.

Sports - pages 6 and 7.

Crossword - Page 8.

Example of *The Easterner*, mentioned in the poem on pages 18 & 19

A Song of Solitude

Sometimes I wonder why
my life goes along
like pieces without the pie.
Every problem seems to multiply
and tumble end over end
as if the sun will never set
or trees will never get
a chance to revel in the wind.

A win is just a stroke of luck
a loss – fragments of inertia.
No matter what the win will cost,
the loss can only hurt you.

A fool will pass it up,
not knowing his own
beginning or end.
What matters is if
his dinner's by six,
clothes are bought,
and every thought of
personal happiness sought.

I try so hard –
reading rules and keeping cool,
not to be the fool.
But sometimes it's difficult to play the stone –
when it erodes and blows away
to play with the sun and stars
and I am so alone.

Seems like the lights
will still turn on and off
and I will still sputter and cough
until I render the end.

I often wonder why
every leaf will leave the tree,
like a man without a friend.
I can only be what I can only be.
And I will face eternity
no matter what
lies around the bend.

(Originally published in *Colors of My Within* and
referenced in the poem *Camping Our Way to Reno* on page 36)

CPSIA information can be obtained
at www.ICGtesting.com
Printed in the USA
FSHW01n1422191018
52987FS